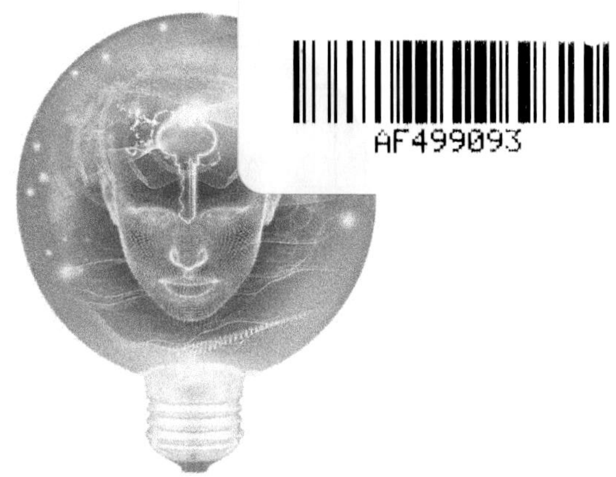

9 Secrets of

Subconscious Mind

For manifesting the desired outcomes

By Dipaali Ghanshyam Patel

www.dipaali.life

DOWNLOAD E-BOOK FOR FREE

Our thoughts and words shape our reality, so it's essential to monitor and transform any negative thoughts before expressing them. Spoken words possess the power to change our destiny. By downloading a free e-book, you can access a list of empowering affirmations designed to counteract negative self-talk. Practicing these affirmations daily, along with utilizing nine manifestation secrets, can help you achieve desired outcomes in all areas of your life.

Click here to download eBook for free:

PREFACE

I am thrilled to share the "9 Secrets of the Subconscious Mind" with all readers and learners. By using this book as a workbook, I can guarantee you 100% results for a better life. These secrets greatly aided me when I faced challenges in relationships, health, and wealth. Thanks to the "9 Secrets," I was able to achieve remarkable breakthroughs.

During my learning journey, I have come across the 9 secrets of the mind through different courses, self-help books, and live workshops. Implementing these secrets into my own life has brought about positive results, and I have also shared them with others to help them manifest their desired outcomes. It has been astonishing to witness how both my students and I have achieved remarkable results in every aspect of life by practicing these 9 secrets. Inspired by this, I have decided to write a book, aiming to share these secrets of the subconscious mind with the world. My ultimate goal is to assist others in effortlessly and gracefully achieving their desired results in life.

I express my deep gratitude to my parents, gurus, family, friends, fellow DDLC learners, and my sons Vasu and Nishith. I would like to offer a special thanks to my husband, whose unwavering support has been invaluable throughout my endeavors. I am also grateful to my daughter Dr. Kripa, who has been a constant presence in my life, always ready to assist me. She played a crucial role in the process of writing, editing, and designing my book. Lastly, I want to acknowledge my mentor, Som Bathla sir, for his guidance and for helping me become a successful author.

Dear reader, welcome to this life-changing workbook that will empower you to redesign your life with ease and effectiveness. This book is specifically designed for individuals who are truly committed to creating a brighter future. Whether you are a professional, entrepreneur, housewife, or student, this book will prove beneficial to you.

The book is divided into two parts for your convenience. The first part delves into "9 Secrets and their Practical Uses," while the second part provides "5 Step Formulas to Make 9 Secrets Successful." To maximize the benefits of this book, it is recommended that you read and reread it, and complete all the given assignments. By doing so, you will be able to make practical use of these secrets and transform your life for the better.

Keep Learning, Keep Growing & Keep Sharing

Dipaali Ghanshyam Patel
Author & Life Coach

FOREWORD

When Dipaali asked me to write a foreword for her debut book, the title alone piqued my curiosity. The prospect of discovering the 9 secrets enthralled me, as I had previously delved into various books exploring the power of the subconscious mind. Naturally, I was eager to delve deeper into this subject through her work.

While reading her book, I personally had a breakthrough and experienced amazing results. I would like to express my appreciation for her in-depth knowledge on the subject. Until now, I had never been able to grasp the use of these 9 secrets in such a profound way. Through her own learning journey, she discovered and integrated these 9 secrets, ultimately uncovering a 5-step success formula for manifesting desired outcomes. It's truly remarkable. Each secret builds upon the other, and thanks to the 5-step formula, I was finally able to connect the dots and successfully implement all 9 secrets.

In the second part of this book, you will discover a 5-step formula for success. This formula will assist you in recognizing and understanding both "conscious" and "subconscious" limiting beliefs. The author has included practical methods within this book to help you identify these beliefs effectively. By addressing your limiting beliefs first, you will be better prepared to manifest the desired results in all aspects of your life.

Each chapter includes assignments that allow you to apply your knowledge to real-life situations. By completing these assignments, you will be able to learn and achieve the desired results in your life with ease and effectiveness.

Best wishes to Dipaali

From Dr. Shailesh Thaker

Author of 64 Books

Content

INTRODUCTION

Are you seeking self-improvement? Do you believe that you deserve a more fulfilling life? If your answer is yes, then you will discover nine incredible secrets in this book that will help you manifest the desired outcomes in your life.

Many individuals attempt to heal or improve their lives by utilizing affirmations or meditation. They often engage in writing down their desired goals, yet find themselves unsatisfied with the outcomes. I personally experienced this as well. For years, I diligently practiced ready-made affirmations and explored various modalities in an effort to heal my own life. While I did see some progress, I found that I remained reactive and continued to think and behave in the same patterns when faced with challenging situations.

Unfortunately, my wisdom seemed ineffective in such circumstances, particularly when dealing with unsupportive individuals.

Are you going through the same thing I went through earlier? If so, make sure to not only read this book, but also complete all the assignments at the end of each chapter. Think of this book as a workbook that will teach you new techniques in every chapter. You can then apply these tools and techniques right away by working on the assignments provided at the end of each chapter.

Using pre-made affirmations created by someone else is comparable to receiving a generic medical treatment for a specific health condition. It is crucial to identify and address your own specific limiting beliefs or issues in order to make progress.

When I discovered the significance of the 9 secrets and realized that understanding the science behind the "5 step formulas" was crucial for their effectiveness, I was able to uncover my conscious and subconscious limiting beliefs. Once I identified these beliefs, it became much simpler for me to address them using these 9 secrets. As a result, my life began to transform. I started seeing positive changes not only in my relationships, but in all other areas of my life as well!

This book provides you with the chance to recognize your conscious and subconscious limiting beliefs. It also teaches you a scientific method to eliminate these beliefs first. Additionally, it prepares you to apply the 9 Secrets of the Subconscious Mind later on. Throughout the book, you'll find numerous practical examples, techniques, stories, authentic breakthrough outcomes, and assignments to help you in your journey.

As you read this book, your mind will undergo a rewiring process that will equip you to intentionally train your mind in order to achieve your desired outcomes in daily life.

Consciously choosing positive thoughts is an intentional decision that requires regular practice in order to train the subconscious mind consistently.

Prepare yourself to manifest the results you desire by utilizing the 9 secrets of the subconscious mind.

Chapter 1, The Power of the Subconscious Mind

"You have to train your mind like you train your body."

-Bruce Jenner

How many things do you see, touch, and observe in a day? How many people do you meet in a day? And how many words do you hear in a day? Have you ever been able to recall all your thoughts from a whole day? We have countless thoughts, meet numerous people, and experience different situations and events every day. All of these are stored in our minds. Some events, experiences, and feelings are temporarily stored and later forgotten, while others are stored for the long term. The information we forget after some time is stored in our conscious mind, while the information we remember for a long time is stored in our subconscious mind.

Our human brain is divided into two parts mainly the conscious mind and the subconscious mind. The conscious mind is active from the moment we wake up in the morning. It helps us make decisions, discern right from wrong, and think logically. Research suggests that the conscious mind only holds about 5% of the power in running our lives, while the remaining 95% is attributed to the subconscious mind.

The subconscious mind, unlike the conscious mind, does not possess the ability to think logically or make decisions. It operates non-stop and lacks the capability to determine what is right or wrong. Instead, it simply processes information based on what it receives through daily events and experiences. All events and experiences first approach the conscious mind, which then evaluates and assesses the information. The conscious mind has the authority to either discard or allow the information to enter the subconscious mind. If an event or experience is deemed significant or shocking, it is immediately stored within our subconscious mind.

On average, humans have over 60,000 thoughts and experience numerous events in a single day. However, the majority of these events are forgotten by the end of the day. Fortunately, our conscious mind serves as a protective barrier for our subconscious mind, filtering out unnecessary thoughts and experiences. This is a blessing, as our subconscious mind lacks the ability to distinguish between positive and negative information. If all the information from a day were directly stored in our subconscious mind, we would become overwhelmed and confused when navigating the real world. Thank goodness for our conscious mind's discerning abilities!

You have observed that sometimes, your subconscious mind surprises you with your own behaviors in certain situations. Have you ever wondered why this happens? It occurs because your subconscious mind is triggered and operates on autopilot, utilizing all the information it has. Always remember that your subconscious mind simply executes. If you have had negative experiences with a particular person, group, or community for a specific task or period of time, and it has influenced your subconscious mind, then the next time you encounter a similar situation, person, or community, your subconscious mind will be primed to adopt specific behaviors. Sometimes, you may witness a person displaying aggressive behavior in some tasks, places, situations, or circumstances, while being gentle and polite with others at the same time. Would you like to understand the reasons behind these contrasting behaviors and beliefs in the same individual? Let's delve into the "3E" principles.

3E Principles

Human brain has adopted behavior based on “3E”: Education, Environment and Experience.

Education

Throughout the day, your subconscious mind is constantly being educated, whether directly or indirectly. It receives and stores information. To illustrate this, let's consider an example.

When I was a child, I used to watch my grandmother give "Prasad" (Satvik Food for God) to my grandfather for his worship. He would then distribute the same "Prasad" to the poor and hungry people sitting near the temple. My grandfather only used flowers and water for his worship. As a child, I observed this entire process, but didn't understand it. One day, I asked my mother to explain it to me. She told me that my grandfather was doing a wonderful thing. God doesn't need food; he needs our love and faith. It is the poor and hungry people who need food. This experience taught me a new way to worship God. It educated my mind and instilled in me the belief that whenever I encounter poor people, I should offer them food, water, and clothes. I simply bow down to God and offer my love and faith to him.

Your subconscious mind unknowingly absorbs unwanted behavior patterns or beliefs as well.

I have a vivid memory of one Sunday afternoon when my father wanted to take a rest. He specifically instructed my mother not to disturb him for the next few hours. To ensure his privacy, my mother locked his bedroom door from the outside. While my father was resting, his best friend, Uncle Rohan, came to our house and knocked on the door. Uncle Rohan wanted to know where my father was, so I told him, "My father said he is neither at home nor resting in the bedroom." Uncle Rohan chuckled and hurried towards the bedroom. This little incident concluded here, but it left a lasting impact on my young mind.

It indirectly taught me an invaluable lesson – that I can lie not only to my best friend, but to anyone else as well, and that it is acceptable to do so.

Every significant event in life has a direct or indirect educational impact. The subconscious mind continually forms new neurological pathways, each with its own set of behaviors and beliefs. While some of these pathways contribute to our personal growth, others do not.

There are couple of questions to introspect.

1. Do you remember any past significant events which are leading you powerfully in the present?

2. Do you remember any past significant event which doesn't serve for better in the present?

3. What are your current beliefs and behaviors when it comes to dealing with difficult people or challenging circumstances?
4. What are your current beliefs and behaviors when it comes to interacting with positive people or favorable situations?

Identify and document significant events that have shaped the neurological pathways responsible for the formation of your beliefs and subsequent behaviors.

It would be helpful if you could pinpoint one specific event that has influenced your current beliefs and behaviors.

ENVIRONMENT

We have no control over the selection of our parents, city, country, and community. These are bestowed upon us at birth. Our name, religion, nationality, gender, and family are assigned to us. We are raised in a particular environment where we inherit food habits, language, clothing culture, behaviors, and beliefs. Our surroundings shape the neurological pathways that define who we are. Often, we carry beliefs from our childhood that we have never truly encountered or that do not align with our practical realities.

For instance, some individuals embrace the enjoyment of non-vegetarian cuisine as a normal part of their lives, while others do not indulge in such food. Similarly, certain individuals feel comfortable wearing Western attire, whereas others do not. Abusive language is accepted by some individuals as a natural aspect of life, while others find it unacceptable. In certain religions, a white wedding gown symbolizes auspiciousness, while in another religion, it is worn by widows. From a young age, we are exposed to a plethora of information that shapes our identity. Our environment plays a crucial role in shaping who we are. Our beliefs regarding money, relationships, health, nation, politics, God, society, people, career, job, business, and the world are formed based on this information, and they become deeply ingrained in our subconscious mind. These beliefs continue to influence us throughout our lives.

What are your beliefs in the areas of

- Health?
- Wealth?

- Relationship?
- Career?

Identify your two-three beliefs and write them down in your notebook. We will discuss more about our beliefs in section 2.

EXPERIENCE

We not only deal with a person but also with their beliefs

We are not only meeting the people, but also meeting their beliefs and attitude.

Have you ever had an experience where you encountered someone for the first time, but you judged and treated them based solely on your own preconceived notions? Alternatively, have you ever been on the receiving end of such treatment, where someone formed opinions about you based on someone else's perceptions?

This is known as experience-based behavior. Our mind relies on past experiences to guide our actions in present situations.

For instance, I received exceptional service at the Bank of America, which has instilled positive beliefs about the bank in my mind. Now, imagine how my behavior will be when I visit the bank again. Without a doubt, it will be positive! Whenever I go to any branch of the Bank of America, I bring my positive experiences with me and conduct myself accordingly. I enter the bank with a positive mindset, and I am even willing to endure certain difficulties for this particular bank. Past experiences will undoubtedly influence my current interaction with the same bank. Now, let's consider the opposite scenario in terms of experience.

I had a terrible experience with a cab driver. He was late, didn't arrive on time, the car was dirty, and his driving was rough. I felt scared and shocked. Not only did this bad experience affect my perception of that specific cab driver, but it also influenced how I view the entire community of drivers and the cab company. As a result, I have made the decision to avoid traveling alone by cab in unfamiliar cities. Even if I do plan to travel by cab with someone else in the future, I know that my state of mind will be filled with fear, anger, or extreme caution. I will choose the cab and its driver very carefully because my mind tells me that I don't feel safe or comfortable at all. My mind reacts to such situations based on past experiences.

We not only encounter individuals, but also interact with their beliefs, which are shaped by their past experiences, upbringing, environment, and education.

In general, our experiences shape the truth of our lives, and we wholeheartedly believe in them. Our subconscious mind, unwaveringly loyal, acts in accordance with the information it holds.

Now, we have identified the reasons behind the contrasting behaviors and beliefs exhibited by the same individual. It is important to note that a person's behavior is shaped by their past experiences, education, and environment. While we may not have the ability to immediately alter our environment, we do have the opportunity to modify our past experiences and education. So, what steps should we take in order to achieve this? How can we identify the chance to cease registering unfavorable experiences and education in our subconscious mind? To answer these questions, it is necessary to delve deeper into the workings of the subconscious mind.

HOW DOES SUBCONSCIOUS MIND WORK?

Let's gain a better understanding of what the subconscious mind is and how it functions by exploring a short story.

A young boy from a hometown decides to travel to another city. He begins his journey on foot and must pass through a dense jungle in order to reach his destination. However, once inside the jungle, he loses his way and is unable to find an exit.

Despite his best efforts, the young boy spends the entire day searching for a way out, but to no avail.

The young boy, feeling tired, decided to rest for the night. He came across a large banyan tree and settled down beneath it. As soon as he sat down, he realized he was hungry, a fact he hadn't noticed all day. Longing for a taste of his home-cooked meals, he was surprised to find fresh, homemade food magically appear before him. Shocked, he couldn't believe his eyes. Although he questioned whether he was dreaming, the reality of the situation dawned on him as he indulged in the meal. His hunger satisfied, he then found himself craving water. To his amazement, water materialized before him. Startled, he cautiously checked to ensure it wasn't an illusion and confirmed its authenticity. Quenching his thirst, he shifted his focus to seeking a comfortable bed in a safe home. Remarkably, he discovered a small, secure dwelling with a cozy bed. Intrigued, he entered the home and lay down on the bed. Now relaxed, at rest, and content, he pondered the extraordinary occurrences of finding food, water, a home, and a comfortable bed in the midst of the dense jungle. Perplexed, he began to connect his experience with a childhood tale of ghosts residing in a tree within the jungle.

As soon as his mind began to connect his experiences with the story of Ghost, panic washed over him. He believed that the ghosts dwelling in the tree had granted his every desire, but now they would plot to kill him as soon as he fell asleep. This is where the story takes a surprising twist - the young boy actually dies immediately after succumbing to panic.

Here, we have several questions about this story. Did the ghosts actually live on the tree? Was their intention to harm the young boy? Absolutely not! In fact, there were no ghosts on the big banyan tree. The banyan tree was a "Kalpvriksh" (a wish-fulfilling tree). Whenever someone sat under that banyan tree and made a wish or thought about something, all their wishes came true.

The young boy sat under the tree, wishing for food, water, safety, a home, and comfort in his life. Surprisingly, his wishes were granted, yet he remained fearful and preoccupied with thoughts of death. Tragically, he passed away in the very next moment.

Do similar things occur in our own lives? Typically, we tend to receive what we consistently think about and desire. However, in reality, we often unintentionally focus our thoughts and conversations on what we truly do not want, and as a result, we ultimately experience the same outcomes in our lives, as depicted in this story. The young boy, without realizing it, fixated on death, and tragically, he perished.

Is your current situation in the areas of health, wealth, relationships, and career a direct or indirect result of your thoughts and desires?

We keep saying what we don't want, as if it will lead us to what we do want.

- Dipaali

Do you intentionally find success and happiness, or have you unknowingly obtained them? Do you consciously consider yourself worthy, or do you become so by chance? Do you believe that you have unintentionally attracted failure, unhappiness in relationships, and an unhealthy body?

Examine the balance sheet of your life and you will see this truth! While it is true that nobody purposely invites unhappiness, failure, diseases, and negative people and situations into their lives, it is our thoughts and desires that contribute to all the suffering in life.

We often find ourselves focusing on what we don't want in life, and interestingly enough, we often end up attracting exactly that. It's important to recognize the influence of our subconscious mind in this process.

Understand the Power of the Subconscious Mind

The subconscious mind can be likened to the "Jinn of the Magical Lamp" as it faithfully carries out all our commands. Just like the Jinn fulfills the wishes of its master, our subconscious mind fulfills our thoughts and desires. It is a gift from God that is bestowed upon every human being, regardless of their appearance, gender, or socio-economic status. Throughout our lives, our subconscious mind is there to fulfill our desires. However, many of us are unaware of how to harness the power of our subconscious mind. We lack the knowledge and understanding of how to effectively communicate with it in order to achieve specific and favorable outcomes.

Default thoughts Vs. Deliberate Positive Thoughts (DT Vs. DPT)

If we fail to purposefully train our subconscious mind in a positive way, it will operate on autopilot. It will rely on all past experiences, both positive and negative. Consider the story of the young boy who unknowingly manifested everything he wanted. He found joy in food and water, security in a house, and solace in his bed where he could rest. Sadly, in the end, his own thoughts and words led to his demise.

Are you a successful, happy, worthy, and healthy individual by mere happenstance? Or are you perhaps unaware of being an unsuccessful, unhappy, and unhealthy individual?

The current situation we find ourselves in is directly influenced by our thoughts and beliefs. Our subconscious mind operates continuously, without pause, and is incredibly faithful. Once our beliefs are embedded in the subconscious mind through significant experiences, it becomes impervious to our conscious directives.

You can understand the concept through your own first bicycle ride. When you were learning to balance on a bicycle, you had to focus on balancing, steering, pedaling, and staying in your lane all at the same time because your subconscious mind wasn't prepared for this new skill. Your mind didn't have any established neurological pathways for this new skill, so you had to put in extra effort to balance and ride the bicycle. Do you remember how much easier it became to ride the bicycle after some conscious effort? This is because your subconscious mind was able to develop new neurological pathways for riding and balancing the bicycle, allowing you to not only balance the bicycle but also ride it hands-free and enjoy the experience.

Likewise, it is important to consistently train your subconscious mind to think positively. Although it may be challenging at first, with regular practice of the "9 Secrets," remarkable outcomes can be achieved. This set of techniques is designed to effortlessly and expeditiously manifest your desires. By incorporating the "9 Secrets" into your life, your subconscious mind will establish fresh, constructive, and influential neural pathways in areas such as health, wealth, relationships, and career.

Gain a thorough understanding of the "9 Secrets" and use them collectively to manifest a single desire. Choose any short-term goal from any aspect of your life. Utilize the bundle of "9 Secrets" as a ritual specifically tailored to that desire. Achieve the desired outcome, confirm its success, celebrate the achievement, and continue to employ these secrets for future desires in your life.

Get ready to uncover the "9 Secrets" of the subconscious mind. To fully grasp these "9 Secrets," read them carefully and complete the accompanying assignments. Make sure to have a notepad and pen handy as you embark on this journey to discover the hidden treasures of your subconscious mind.

"Train your subconscious mind intentionally with positive thoughts; otherwise, it will function by default."

Dipaali

CHAPTER 1, ASSIGNMENT

Note: Please write your answers or actions in the space provided after each task and make full use of it.

Identify and record your beliefs about health (Include both supportive and non-supportive beliefs.)

Identify and record your beliefs about wealth (Include both supportive and non-supportive beliefs.)

____

____

____

____

Identify and record your beliefs about relationships (Include both supportive and non-supportive beliefs.)

____

____

____

____

____

____

Identify and record your beliefs about career (Include both supportive and non-supportive beliefs.)

____

____

____

____

____

____

How does holding non-supportive beliefs affect your current life?

____

____

____

____

How do supportive beliefs guide your path in life?

____

____

____

____

____

What is your understanding of the subconscious mind?

____

____

____

____

____

CHAPTER 2, SECRET #1

Choose your words wisely, for they have the power to shape your reality.

JOLENOR SALIGUMBA

If you're interested in training your subconscious mind with Deliberate Positive Thoughts (DPT), Secret #1, "Affirmation," is crucial. But what exactly is an affirmation? Well, it's quite simple: "Anything you think and say is an affirmation!" You might be wondering about the fact that around 97% of people tend to think and speak negatively about 99% of the time. However, there's no need to delve into the science of affirmation.

In this lesson, you will learn about the "3P" principles, which are effective techniques for affirmations. Before we delve into these principles, please take a moment to write down your desires in each area of your life. This exercise will help you identify your specific desires and give you the opportunity to manifest them. Remember, according to the Law of Nature, you receive what you ask for. So, get ready to ask, be open to receiving, and let the universe work in your favor.

WHAT ARE THE 3P'S?

First "P" - Firstly, when creating your affirmation, ensure that it is in the present tense. Avoid using the past or future tense. Instead, express your desires as if you have already achieved them. Your subconscious mind cannot distinguish between reality and imagination, so affirm and believe that you already possess what you desire in your life.

Second "P" - Ensure that your sentence is framed in a positive manner. Negative words such as "No, Not, Don't, Won't, aren't, isn't, hasn't," etc., do not serve as effective affirmations. Keep in mind the underlying science behind this principle: we attract what we think and talk about. If you express the lack of something, the universe will respond with

"Tathastu" (Your wish is my command). Therefore, always avoid using negative words when formulating your affirmations. Instead, concentrate on clearly stating what you desire.

Third "P" - When creating an affirmation, it is important to make it personal. Ask yourself if you are clear about your desires and who specifically wants them. If the answer is "I," then ensure that your affirmation reflects this. By being specific and using "I," you avoid confusing your subconscious mind. For example, instead of saying "Everyone wants happiness," specify who, in particular, desires happiness. Similarly, if you state "People deserve growth in life!", it is unclear who should be assigned this growth by the subconscious mind.

Most of the time, we tend to think and speak in general terms. However, our mind cannot fulfill our desires unless it understands the specific instructions. Let's consider a scenario: you have visited a restaurant before and have ordered a dish that you specifically wanted. Now, imagine if you were to simply tell the waiter, "Serve me Mexican

Food." In this case, the waiter would have multiple options under the category of "Mexican Food" on the menu. The waiter is always ready to assist, but they need to know the precise dish you desire. Similarly, in life, we often think and communicate in general terms, and as a result, we don't receive what we truly want and deserve. So, are you truly clear about what you want in your life? This is the most important question one can ask oneself. Successful people have a clear understanding of their desires, which is why they are able to effortlessly achieve them. By learning the "9 Secrets" of the subconscious mind, you can create an opportunity to clarify your desires and manifest them easily.

Now let's use the "3P" Principle with the examples and understand them thoroughly.

Example:

1. Everyone wants to earn more money. Or
2. I want to earn $ 10,000 per month.

Which statement is correct? The correct statement is sentence number 2. This is because it follows the "3P" principles. The second sentence meets all the "3P" principles as it is in the present tense, it is positive, and it is a personal statement. On the other hand, sentence number 1 is a general statement, and it is unclear who it refers to, making it difficult for the reader to understand.

Now, apply or review the "3P" principles to your affirmation. Have you incorporated the "3P" principles in your affirmation? Do you believe that example number 2 is a suitable example of an affirmation?

I want to announce that while sentence number 2 contains the "3P" principles, it is not a correct example of affirmation. Using the word "want" in an affirmation won't work, and you won't be able to manifest what you desire in your life.

Once again, let's examine the same example to enhance our understanding.

"I ***want*** to earn $10,000 per month."

Remove the word "want" from this sentence, and your affirmation is ready to serve you.

Correct affirmation:

- ***"I earn $ 10,000 per month."***

Please correct your statement by removing the word "want" and constructing it correctly.

Now, you might be wondering, "Why should we remove the word 'want' from the affirmation?"

You should avoid using the word "want" as it conveys scarcity and lack. When you use "want," it implies that you do not possess it. This word sends an indirect message to your subconscious mind that it desires something it does not currently have. It's important to understand the science behind the subconscious mind – it comprehends and responds to your words, thoughts, and beliefs. While "want" may help you clarify your desires, it does not contribute to fulfilling them. Instead, construct your affirmations by assuming that you already possess what you desire, and you will undoubtedly attain it.

In order to construct a correct affirmation, it is important to avoid using words such as "should," "must," "would," "can," "could," "may," and "wish," as they all have similar meanings to the word "want." Instead, practice the "3P" Principles.

Let's take a look at three examples in each area of life!

Examples:

Health:

1. I have perfect health.
2. I have perfect body weight.
3. My body heals faster.

Wealth

1. I earn $10,000 per month.
2. I am financially free.
3. I have multiple passive income streams.

Relationships

1. I have wonderful relationships with my parents.
2. I love my husband & he is very loving & caring.
3. I have great bond with my children.

Career

1. I have very supportive people at my workplace.
2. My happy clients love to recommend my services to others.
3. I have always great opportunity to grow in my profession and I am growing every day.

In your notepad, make sure to create at least 3 affirmations for each area of your life. Don't be concerned about your current circumstances. Instead, focus on determining what you truly need, applying the principles of "3P". Try to avoid using words like "want," "would," "could," "should," "can," and so on. Once you have established the appropriate affirmations, your subconscious mind will begin to receive signals. By consciously directing your subconscious mind through affirmations, it will support you at the right moment.

Affirmation is the language that speaks to your subconscious mind. If you don't know how to communicate with it, how can your subconscious mind understand what you truly desire? Our subconscious mind is always eager to assist us, but we lack knowledge of the communication methods it understands. Affirmation serves as the universal language between our conscious and subconscious minds. By consciously using the right affirmations to communicate with your subconscious mind, it will joyfully and effectively support you. Additionally, affirmations aid in transforming your inner dialogues. Therefore, utilize affirmations for a more fulfilling life. Happy writing of affirmations!

Chapter 2, Assignment

Note: Please write your answers or actions in the space provided after each task and make full use of it.

Create a comprehensive wish list that includes all areas of your life.

Create three affirmations for the area of Health applying the 3P principle for assistance.

____

____

____

____

____

____

Create three affirmations for the area of Wealth applying the 3P principle for assistance.

____

____

____

____

Create three affirmations for the area of Relationships applying the 3P principle for assistance.

____

____

____

____

____

Create three affirmations for the area of Career applying the 3P principle for assistance.

____

____

____

____

____

CHAPTER 3, SECRET #2

"Gratitude can transform common days into thanksgivings, turn routine jobs into joy, and change ordinary opportunities into blessings."

William Arthur Ward

Congratulations! You have mastered the art of creating accurate affirmations. With this skill, you can effectively communicate your desires to your subconscious mind, and it will work for you in the right time and place. However, creating correct affirmations alone is not sufficient for manifesting your desired outcomes in life. In fact, it is just one small part - 1/9, to be exact - of the entire manifestation process.

Do you believe you deserve a better life? Do you think you can positively redesign your life at any time? Do you feel that you can improve in every area of your life, but find yourself stuck? If so, then secret #2 is the Master Key! It's like salt! Just imagine your dish looking amazing with all the ingredients, but lacking salt! Would you be able to eat that dish? Could you truly enjoy that food? No, not at all! Similarly, if you create accurate affirmations but fail to include "Gratitude" in them, they won't be effective. Your affirmation is like a skeleton without "Gratitude". If you want to breathe life into your affirmations, show your gratitude. Intentionally include the word "Gratitude" in your affirmations, and they will come to life.

Gratitude holds immense power as it has the ability to instantly shift our mindset from negative to positive. Expressing gratitude towards others has the remarkable effect of melting away our ego, grounding us, and elevating our positive state of mind. The saying "Gratitude is the best attitude!" holds true and should be embraced in our daily lives. It is vital to recognize that if we fail to appreciate what we have, we may lose it. This is a fundamental principle of nature. By cultivating a habit of gratitude towards everyone we encounter, we enhance our own worth, happiness, and well-being. The natural order responds to our gratitude and rewards us abundantly.

Imagine that when guests visit your home and you warmly receive them, they will be more inclined to connect with you in the future. Conversely, if you fail to welcome them with happiness, they will be less likely to visit you again. Similarly, by expressing gratitude at every opportunity, you will enhance your worth, happiness, and overall well-being.

By reading this, you may be thinking, "I always say 'Thank You' to everyone, so why am I not getting what I want in life?" It's a valid question. And I have a question to answer yours: "Do you truly mean it?" In most cases, the answer is no. Often, we say "Thank you!" without genuine sincerity. It has become a robotic habit for us. We don't even make eye contact when expressing gratitude. But is this the right way to practice gratitude? No, it is not. To truly reap the immense benefits of gratitude, you need to use Secret #2 - Gratitude - correctly.

Let's dive into a captivating story! Mr. Sharma worked at the "Cold Storage" facility as an engineer. His responsibility was to regulate the temperature in the "cold storage cabins" alongside his colleagues. Every morning, Mr. Sharma would enter the cold storage cabin with a delightful smile and greet the gatekeeper. In the evenings, as he left the cabin, he would sincerely express his gratitude by saying "Thank you" to the gatekeeper. This kind gesture from Mr. Sharma always brought joy to the gatekeeper, and they developed an unconscious rapport. The gatekeeper eagerly anticipated Mr. Sharma's warm greetings in the mornings and his gratefulness in the evenings. Numerous engineers would pass by the gate where the gatekeeper stood, but they never acknowledged him or his duty.

One evening, the gatekeeper noticed that Mr. Sharma hadn't shown sincere gratitude. Although the cold-storage cabin was locked and all employees had left, Mr. Sharma had not returned. Concerned, the gatekeeper decided to search for him. With the key to the cabin, he opened the door where the temperature was minus 15 degrees Celsius. His intention was to find Mr. Sharma, who had greeted him warmly in the morning but failed to express gratitude in the evening. While searching, the gatekeeper called out Mr. Sharma's name loudly. Eventually, he discovered Mr. Sharma unconscious on the cold floor inside the cabin, nearly frozen. Acting quickly, the gatekeeper pulled him out and provided initial treatment, which helped him regain consciousness. Mr. Sharma expressed gratitude to the gatekeeper for saving his life. The next day, the cold-storage company commended the gatekeeper for his actions and compassion, asking him to share his account of the incident. The gatekeeper stated that he hadn't done anything for Mr. Sharma. It was Mr. Sharma's attitude of gratitude that reminded him of his absence in the evening. He explained that he couldn't keep track of every employee's records and couldn't have saved Mr. Sharma's life. It was Mr. Sharma's own attitude of gratitude that saved him. This illustrates the power of gratitude—an attitude that can win the hearts of many.

Expressing sincere gratitude has the power to forge meaningful connections and bring about lasting positive outcomes in life. Not only does it spread happiness, but it also brings joy to both the giver and the recipient. Gratitude has a contagious effect, as expressing appreciation often prompts others to reciprocate with their own gratitude. It is a portable sentiment that can be carried with us at all times, without the need for any special permission. There is no need to wait for the perfect moment or the right people to show our gratitude. By expressing appreciation, we open doors to new opportunities and foster personal growth. Embrace gratitude, for it holds the key to personal development and a fulfilling life!

I have observed that there are many people who fail to appreciate what they have in their lives.

Consequently, they find it difficult to attain happiness, good health, and financial prosperity. It is crucial to cultivate gratitude in order to achieve everything in life. Despite our desires for more, we often neglect to express gratitude. However, gratitude holds immense power. By practicing gratitude, one can swiftly and effortlessly reap the rewards.

Let us begin embracing an attitude of gratitude from this day forward, purposefully integrating it into our lives, and remaining open to the endless possibilities of creating miracles!

We should express our deep gratitude to many individuals, locations, and circumstances. We should be grateful for our good health and for the various products and electronic devices that enhance our daily lives. Moreover, we should appreciate having access to fresh food, clean air, and safe water. Additionally, we should truly be thankful for the clothing, shelter, sunlight, and financial resources that we possess. Let us not forget to acknowledge the support we receive from those around us, as well as the government that provides us with identification. We should also recognize the contributions of organizations, educational institutions, hospitals, doctors, accountants, lawyers, engineers, scientists, car manufacturers, airlines, farmers, store owners, artists, internet providers, teachers, parents, sanitation workers, electricity providers, internet service providers, libraries, authors, dairy farmers, chefs, restaurants, hotels, clothing merchants, fashion designers, jewelry stores, skilled employees, gardeners, car washers, drivers, security personnel, and administrative staff, among many others.

Have you ever considered the unconditional contributions they make in our lives? Often, we overlook their presence. From now on, let's start acknowledging their daily impact on our lives. Remember to be grateful for everything you have and everything you do.

You can practice gratitude in two ways. First, show gratitude for everything you have in your life! This is crucial, as acknowledging your worth and expressing gratitude is essential for personal growth.

Assignment: Daily Gratitude List

Make a daily list of six new things that you are grateful for!

I am grateful for .... because ....

Example:

I am grateful for my home because it provides me with the comfort and safety I need.

Not only should you show gratitude towards people, places, products, and circumstances, but you should also identify the reasons why you are grateful for them. Make it a daily practice and keep an exclusive journal for your Daily Gratitude List. Identify six new events, people, places, and products that have positively impacted your life and helped you grow. Don't forget to include non-favorable people, events, products, places, and circumstances as well. They should also be part of your Daily Gratitude List because we can actually learn and evolve more from them than from the favorable ones. If we exclude them, the power of gratitude doesn't work for us. Show sincere gratitude to everyone who has contributed to your life, directly or indirectly, whether it's in a supportive or non-supportive way. Find the positive lessons in non-favorable situations and people, and express gratitude towards them as well.

Example:

I had always dreamed of becoming a doctor, but I was unable to continue my studies in the science stream. Despite being a brilliant student, certain circumstances forced me to switch from science to commerce. While many of my friends, who were average performers in school, went on to become doctors, I ended up with a commerce degree. I felt unhappy and constantly compared myself to them, complaining about my career to my family.

However, my path has led me to become a life coach, where I am able to offer love, wisdom, and compassion to humanity. Through my contributions, millions of people can instantly and positively transform their lives. Connecting the dots in my career brings me great satisfaction. I believe that God always has a greater plan. I sincerely thank God that circumstances prevented me from becoming a doctor at that time, as it has allowed me to spread happiness, offer hope, and teach formulas for a simple and successful life.

My past difficulties have given me the opportunity to make a meaningful impact on the lives of millions through my talks, YouTube videos, books, online school, and podcasts. In any other profession, I would not have been able to achieve this. Therefore, I now understand how to show gratitude for those unfavorable circumstances from the past. Here, I would like to demonstrate how I practice this gratitude:

- *I am extremely grateful to God for becoming a life coach, as it allows me to share my love, wisdom, and compassion with humanity. Thank you, thank you, thank you!*

For the next 21 days, make sure to include both positive and negative aspects of circumstances, people, situations, places, events, and products in your "Daily Gratitude List." Show genuine gratitude and prepare for a promising future. It is essential to let go of any unfinished business or grievances from the past in order to move forward in life. Gratitude has the power to release you from all your resentments. If you want to advance in your journey, open the doors to happiness and success with the Master Key of Gratitude.

Once you begin regularly practicing the Daily Gratitude List to acknowledge and appreciate what you have in your life, it is now the perfect time to move on to part 2 of Gratitude, which will help you create a vibrant future for yourself.

Choose one area of your life and select an affirmation that you created in Chapter 1. Let's now embark on creating a bright future by utilizing Secret #2 - Gratitude. I have chosen my career as the area of focus and will be using one affirmation in conjunction with Secret #2.

For Example:

Secret #1,

- *I earn $10,000 per month.*

This affirmation is correct for the career area. Now, I will apply Secret #2 to manifest it more quickly. Remember, we are designing our future using the "9 Secrets." So, whatever you desire for your future, imagine that you have already accomplished it and express gratitude for it.

For example:

Secret #1 & #2,

- *I am incredibly grateful to be earning $10,000 per month.*

When you incorporate the word "Grateful" into your affirmation, you profoundly impact your neurological pathways. This sentence becomes dynamic and ready to work in your favor. By affirming and expressing gratitude simultaneously, you acknowledge that you have already received what you desire. Our subconscious mind lacks logical reasoning and cannot verify the accuracy of stored information. However, this limitation presents an opportunity for us. We can consciously communicate our desires to the subconscious mind. Begin by applying the "3P" principle and incorporating the word "Gratitude" to affirm your future in the present moment. This practice will undoubtedly manifest your desires in life. Enhance all the affirmations you crafted in chapter #2 by infusing them with "Gratitude.".

For example,

Health:

1. I am ***grateful*** to have perfect health.

2. I am ***grateful*** to have perfect body weight.
3. I am ***grateful*** that my body heals faster.

Wealth:

1. I am ***grateful*** to earn $10,000 per month consistently.
2. I am ***grateful*** for my financial freedom.
3. I am ***grateful*** to have multiple passive income streams.

Relationships:

1. I am so ***grateful*** to have wonderful relationships with my parents.
2. I love my husband & I am ***grateful*** for having a loving and caring husband.

3. I am ***grateful*** to have great bond with my children.

Career:

1. I am ***grateful*** to have very supportive people at my workplace.

2. I am ***grateful*** for recommendation of my happy clients for my services and online courses.
3. I am ***grateful*** to God, that I always have a great opportunity to grow in my profession, and I am growing every day.

You can express gratitude by using the word "Gratitude" or by showing appreciation to specific individuals or situations, such as your God, Gurus, Employers, Parents, Friends, Family members, or your children. Now is the perfect time to bring your affirmation to life by utilizing the power of Gratitude, which is Secret #2

Chapter 3, Assignment

Note: Please write your answers or actions in the space provided after each task and make full use of it.

Identify six new things, people, or situations that you have in your life, and cultivate gratitude by creating a "Daily Gratitude List."

Identify negative individuals and circumstances, and make sure to include them in your "Daily Gratitude List." This way, you can express gratitude for the valuable lessons they have taught you.

Identify 10 desires in the area of Health and enhance them by incorporating the word "Gratitude." Show gratitude by recognizing that you have already achieved what you desire in your life.

____

____

____

____

____

____

____

____

____

____

____

Identify 10 desires in the area of Wealth and enhance them by incorporating the word "Gratitude." Show gratitude by recognizing that you have already achieved what you desire in your life.

____

____

____

____

____

____

____

____

____

____

Identify 10 desires in the area of Relationships and enhance them by incorporating the word "Gratitude." Show gratitude by recognizing that you have already achieved what you desire in your life.

____

____

____

____

____

____

____

____

____

____

____

Identify 10 desires in the area of Career and enhance them by incorporating the word "Gratitude." Show gratitude by recognizing that you have already achieved what you desire in your life.

____

____

____

____

____

____

____

____

____

____

____

Practice gratitude in your daily life by sincerely expressing gratitude to at least three people, places, or situations each day.

____

____

____

____

____

____

____

____

____

____

____

CHAPTER 4, SECRET #3

"Feel it, Achieve it!"

– Dipaali

Do you want to achieve results that are ten times greater than what you are currently producing? While affirmations and sincere gratitude are commonly practiced, they often do not produce significant results within a specific timeframe. For instance, let's say I want to earn $10,000 per month and I regularly practice affirmations while expressing gratitude for this desired income. Such practices assist in reorienting my mindset towards money and career, but they do not accelerate the manifestation of desired outcomes in life. If you are seeking rapid results and tenfold growth in your life, you must go beyond simply affirming your goals – you need to truly embody and experience them.

We initially start practicing affirmations with the goal of manifesting something in our lives. However, over time, it can unknowingly become a ritual. I have observed many individuals who excel at creating affirmations and are dedicated to practicing them daily. Yet, as time goes on, it becomes monotonous. Some people even write each affirmation 21 times, twice a day, yet surprisingly, they do not see any results. They end up with stacks of notebooks filled with affirmations. While practicing affirmations is a part of their lives and can help create new neurological pathways, it is a slow process. Our subconscious mind perceives these daily written affirmations as a ritual, similar to brushing our teeth, taking a bath, or eating meals. It becomes an automated habit without any real meaning to our subconscious mind. As a result, our subconscious mind does not receive the command to fulfill these affirmations unless we truly FEEL them.

We often observe individuals who devoutly worship their God through chanting, reading holy books, and adhering to commandments day after day, year after year. But are these individuals truly happy, healthy, and deserving of their faith? Do they truly embody peace and compassion? Are they proactive, grounded, and serene? Do they genuinely comprehend the words they recite and understand the significance of their daily rituals? How many people can truly transform their lives through the practice of chanting or reading holy books? The answer, unfortunately, is very few. This is primarily because many simply follow the traditions of their parents, family, community, or spiritual leaders without grasping the deeper purpose behind these rituals. While chanting and obeying commandments can indeed have positive effects on one's well-being and prosperity, why do these individuals fail to bring about any significant positive changes in their lives? The answer lies in their oversight of a crucial element of manifestation: the power of truly feeling and embracing their beliefs.

If you practice your daily affirmations without feeling them, you won't see faster results. Similarly, if you chant or read the holy book without truly connecting to the words, how can your subconscious mind create new neurological pathways? How will it be able to replace old limiting beliefs with positive ones?

Feel it, no matter what you think or say. This is crucial. Without feeling it, you cannot succeed. Emotions are strong signals to our subconscious mind. It doesn't care about your native language. It doesn't matter how intelligent and articulate you are, or how dedicated you are to practicing affirmations in your daily life. Your subconscious mind pays attention to your feelings, how you feel when you think and speak. Are you joyful, enthusiastic, sad, annoyed, or upset? Your feelings communicate with your subconscious mind faster than your words.

As human beings, we are inherently emotional. Our thoughts, words, and actions are always accompanied by feelings. While we may forget specific dialogues or situations from movies, we never forget the emotions we experienced during those moments. Our subconscious mind has a remarkable ability to connect with our emotions and retain them for a significant period of time. It is through this direct connection that emotions have the ability to greatly impact our lives, serving as a powerful tool for both creation and destruction.

Emotions are everything!

Now, get ready to utilize this powerful tool to build a positive life for yourself. You can accomplish this by incorporating vibrational words into your affirmations. Intentionally introduce these vibrational words into your subconscious mind and truly experience their impact. Initially, you may not genuinely feel the emotions associated with these words, but keep going until you make it. Gradually, you will undoubtedly start feeling genuine excitement, happiness, contentment, and confidence towards your desired affirmations.

Example:

- I am ***grateful*** to earn $10,000 per month consistently.

The statement above encompasses the initial two secrets. It is currently active and prepared to assist you, albeit in its infancy. To facilitate its development and enhance its ability to help us materialize our desired outcomes, it requires nourishment. Identify a single word that resonates with you on a vibrational level, one that ignites joy and enthusiasm, and incorporate that word into the aforementioned statement.

Example:

- I am so ***glad*** and grateful to earn $ 10,000 per month.

Your affirmation is now even more powerful and effective when you intentionally include a vibrational word.

Take a moment to reread all of your statements below and observe the remarkable difference it makes.

1. I ***want*** to earn $ 10,000 per month consistently.
2. I earn $ 10,000 per month consistently.
3. I am ***grateful*** to earn $ 10,000 per month consistently.
4. I am ***glad*** & grateful to earn $ 10,000 per month consistently.

Which statement is vibrating? Statement number 4. When you read statement number 4, your vibrational word consciously reminds your subconscious mind that you feel glad, happy, and excited. Once your subconscious mind receives these signals of happiness, it begins producing chemicals (neurotransmitters) in your body. It starts behaving like a happy and successful individual, bringing a joyful and powerful state of mind. A joyful mind is always prepared for manifestation and open to receiving better results in life. Intentionally put your mind in a happy state, identify vibrational words, create a list of them, and use them frequently in your daily life. Practice affirmations that incorporate these vibrational words.

Example:

HEALTH

1. I am ***amazed*** & grateful to have perfect health.
2. I am ***excited*** & grateful to have perfect body weight.
3. I am ***glad*** & grateful that my body heals faster.

WEALTH

1. I ***feel fantastic*** & grateful to earn $ 10,000 per month consistently.
2. I feel ***relaxed*** & grateful for my financial freedom.
3. I feel ***blessed*** & grateful to have multiple passive income streams.

Relationships

1. I am so **happy** & grateful to have wonderful relationships with my parents.
2. I love my husband & I feel ***complete*** & show my gratitude for having a loving and caring husband.
3. I ***feel joyous*** and I am grateful to have great bond with my children.

Career

1. I ***feel supportive*** and I am grateful to have very supportive people at my workplace.
2. I ***feel happy*** and I am *grateful* for recommendation of my happy clients for my services and online courses.
3. I ***feel blessed*** & grateful to God, that I always have a great opportunity to grow in my profession, and I am growing every day.

Have you noticed the difference? Do you feel a new energy in the statements mentioned earlier? Did you experience excitement, joy, and happiness when you intentionally included vibrational words in your affirmations? By incorporating vibrational words into your affirmations, you can now enhance your ability to feel them.

Congratulations! Your affirmations are now ready to start delivering results. They will work even faster when fueled by your emotions. Remember to add that fuel. Just like a vehicle needs fuel to run or compete on a track, your affirmations require the power of emotions to be effective. Having a Ferrari car is impressive, but it won't get you anywhere without fuel. Similarly, creating the perfect affirmation and practicing it daily is important, but it alone won't produce the desired results. It's like building and assembling a Ferrari – that's just one part of the process. The other crucial part is adding fuel and preparing it for the race. So, let your emotions flow, truly feel it, and redefine YOUR Life!

FEEL GOOD Always!

Chapter 4, Assignment

Note: Please write your answers or actions in the space provided after each task and make full use of it.

Create a compilation of words that convey vibrancy.

Revise your current affirmations by incorporating the term "vibrational."

____

____

____

____

____

____

____

____

____

____

____

____

Incorporate vibrational words into your daily life and experience the positive impact they can make and write your everyday experiences here.

____

____

____

____

____

____

____

____

____

____

____

CHAPTER 5, SECRET #4

"My inner world is creates my outer world."

T. Harv Eker

We validate that our inner world shapes our outer world. Our outer world, in fact, mirrors our internal dialogues that we carry with us in every situation and with every person. Through our five senses (sight, touch, hearing, taste, and smell), our mind receives countless pieces of information. We engage in observation, listening, experiences, and various tasks throughout the day, and all of these activities and experiences are stored in our subconscious mind. Our subconscious mind then utilizes this information as needed, manifesting it in our lives. Essentially, it serves as the default system that governs our existence. At times, we may notice changes in our physicality, voice quality, and responses, compared to our usual routine, when we are not feeling well. For instance, when we are upset, our shoulders slump, our gaze drops, our breathing becomes shallow, and our voice becomes lower in tone.

We have observed that many people share similar physiology, and it is important to comprehend the scientific explanation behind our physiology and inner world. Is there a connection between the two? Why does our physiology undergo changes when we experience happiness or sadness? The answer lies in the direct connection between our body and mind. Our thoughts and emotions can be likened to applications that require an operating system to function. Once we experience something, our body responds accordingly. When we feel motivated and happy, our shoulders become straight and tense, our breathing is either normal or slow, and our voice tonality is normal to high.

NLP (Neuro-Linguistic Programming) teaches us about the connection between physiology and our mindset. According to NLP, our emotions directly influence our body, and our body responds accordingly to the signals it receives from our emotions and thoughts. If this concept holds true for us, it brings good news. If our emotions shape our physiology and our physiology determines our state of mind, then why not utilize this fundamental science to reset our inner compass and manifest the outcomes we desire? Since our body and mind are interconnected, and our emotions and thoughts impact our physiology, let us leverage our physiology to reset our inner compass. It's as simple as that! This is the first key to success, enabling us to swiftly and effortlessly change our state of mind.

Many athletes, stage performers, artists, public figures, and influencers are utilizing this formula to improve their performance. They prepare themselves by setting powerful and relevant physical states, allowing them to excel in their respective fields and achieve the desired results.

Adjust your physiology to achieve the desired results. If you aim to exude confidence, happiness, and success, adopt the physicality associated with being confident, happy, and successful. This nonverbal communication with your subconscious mind will signal that you are confident, happy, and successful, ultimately resetting your inner compass. Rest assured, this formula is both simple and effective.

People often unknowingly adopt a mindset of sadness and failure, typically in response to certain events, individuals, or environments. This mindset then perpetuates their feelings of sadness and failure, leading them to behave and think as if they are inherently unsuccessful.

This state is known as a non-resourceful state, which is influenced by our internal perception. It is dependent on how we view and interpret each situation and individual. Our mind consistently interprets situations and adapts our behaviors accordingly. While external circumstances and experiences have less impact, it is crucial how we internalize them. This ultimately shapes our behavior through our physiology.

Let's understand through a story...

The grandson asked his mom why his grandmother was both emotionally unhappy and in physical pain. His grandmother had such severe pain in her knees that she couldn't walk, which made her sad. Wanting his grandmother to be happy, the grandson worried about her and turned to his mother for ideas on how to bring back her happiness. The mother taught the boy a simple technique, which made him excited and filled with joy. Without wasting any time, he hurried to his grandmother and began using the technique. Within just a few minutes, his grandmother's face lit up with a smile. Not only that, she was able to stand on her own two feet and even started clapping.

What technique did the grandson use to make his grandmother happy and motivated? It is a simple technique called "Resourceful State." The technique involves bringing her into a resourceful state by recalling her past happy memories. He reminded her of joyful and happy events from her life, such as cooking for her family, celebrating festivals together, playing with her grandchildren, or recent family vacations. By reminding her of these happy moments, her mind returned to a resourceful state, which also influenced her behavior. Now, when the mind is reminded of such a powerful and positive state, known as the "Resourceful State" of mind, what obvious physical reactions can one adopt? For his grandmother, standing up, smiling, and clapping were her natural responses. What might yours be? Take a moment to close your eyes and think about it.

Express your emotions through powerful gestures such as swinging your hands in the air, punching your fist on your palm, tapping your legs on the ground, opening up your arms, hugging yourself or a pillow, dancing, running happily, laughing, singing, and raising your head towards the sky, among others.

These gestures are quick, compact, and portable, allowing you to use them anytime and anywhere.

They can help you instantly and effectively enter a resourceful state.

It's really that simple! Just remember, whenever you're feeling sad, upset, fearful, or anxious, you're in a non-resourceful state. The key is to quickly recognize these non-resourceful states and replace them with resourceful ones by using your body language. Assign a specific gesture to help you enter that resourceful state.

Think about how a cricketer celebrates after taking a wicket, or how politicians celebrate a victory. Consider how athletes, stage performers, and successful individuals use gestures to convey their success. A simple gesture can speak volumes. It reflects our internal state. Now, let's adopt the same approach as successful and happy people. In this story, the grandson reminds his grandmother of her happiest moments. It takes her a few minutes to revisit that state of mind. The same applies to everyone.

The first step is to put yourself in a resourceful state by recalling powerful past memories. Our subconscious mind holds a wealth of happy memories that can be used as a reference to bring back happiness and instill confidence and motivation.

If you are unable to enter the "Resourceful" state by recalling strong and impactful memories, you can utilize the second method, known as "Deliberate Powerful Physiology" using the "AS IF" technique.

"AS IF" TECHNIQUE

To improve clarity and flow, use the following steps to deliberately bring yourself into a resourceful state using the "AS IF" technique:

- Stand up.
- Now, take a couple of deep breaths as if you were confident.
- Bring a smile to your face, as if you were an accomplished person.
- Straighten your shoulders and puff out your chest, as if you have achieved success.
- Open your arms and raise your head towards the sky as if expressing gratitude.
- Move from one place to another with excitement.
- Observe the sparks in your eyes, as if you are radiating happiness from within.

- Now, in this position of power and resourcefulness, express your desired affirmations verbally.
- Fire the gesture (physiology) and repeat it again and again.
- Tap into your inner power. Incorporate that particular gesture into your daily routine as often as you can.

The "AS IF" technique is a powerful method to cultivate a state called "Deliberate Powerful Physiology." By adopting this technique, you can send immediate signals to your mind, signaling that you are someone who achieves, is successful, happy, excited, grateful, and always ready to take action. Take a moment to notice the transformation - you are now in a resourceful state, truly prepared to take positive action. Just a few minutes ago, you may have felt hopeless, upset, sad, and worried, but now you are in a completely different state. You have become a powerful being, fully equipped and motivated to take action.

Utilize the "AS IF" technique as a means to conquer anxiety, depression, and fear in life. This technique alters your internal dialogue, revealing fresh perspectives and possibilities. By adopting a joyful and enthusiastic mindset, your mind will generate remarkable solutions to your challenges.

You have two options to access a resourceful state: either establish a specific gesture that instantly brings you into that state, or remind yourself of past joyful and successful moments. Alternatively, you can use the "Deliberate Powerful Physiology" technique by adopting the "AS IF" approach to embody that resourceful state. Always remember the principle of "Like attracts like," as it is a law of nature. If you radiate happiness and genuine joy, you will attract more happiness into your life. Similarly, if you begin by expressing excitement, you will gradually invite more exciting news into your life.

Why is it important to maintain a resourceful state? Why should we adopt a specific gesture? How does this relate to the first three secrets? How can I utilize secret #4, Gesture, to effectively manifest the desired results?

When you cultivate a resourceful state through intentional actions, you become ready to achieve anything you desire in life. Your subconscious mind becomes attuned to signals of victory, joy, happiness, and success.

It is not enough to simply practice affirmations without incorporating gestures. Gestures hold significant power as they validate feelings of success and happiness. While affirming and expressing gratitude with positive words is one aspect, using powerful gestures is another. These gestures demonstrate excitement, happiness, and a celebration of anticipated success, as if you have already achieved or received your desired outcome. Remember, your subconscious mind does not differentiate between the virtual and real worlds. By establishing empowering gestures before encounters with others, performances on stage or at work, or interactions with family members, you will undoubtedly manifest your desires.

I have observed many individuals who engage in practices such as affirmations, incorporating positive words, and expressing gratitude. However, I have noticed that their actions often seem mechanical and lacking genuine emotion. These individuals have conditioned themselves to believe that happiness is only attainable once they achieve success. Unfortunately, this mindset is flawed and will never lead to true fulfillment. If we are not genuinely happy and fail to demonstrate happiness through our actions, we will not achieve the success we desire in life. Our actions and gestures serve as a representation of our inner state. Our subconscious mind does not discriminate based on our native language. Regardless of whether we are Japanese, German, Indian, or American and use different languages to communicate externally, our subconscious mind only understands the language of our physiology. This language is universal and serves as a powerful means of communication with our subconscious mind.

To establish your gesture, you have several options. You can punch your fist into another hand, wave your hand in the air, shout while pushing both hands back, give a high five, dance, jump, or adopt a warrior pose, Superman pose, or Wonder Woman pose. Choose a gesture that feels comfortable for you, either consciously or by recalling past powerful memories, and then affirm your desired statement. Remember to include a vibrational word and express gratitude within it.

For instance, I thrust my fist into another hand, replenish my resourceful state, and vocalize it aloud:

"I am incredibly glad and grateful to be earning $10,000 per month. And every time I think about it, my mind responds with a resounding "Yes, yes, yes, you are indeed earning $10,000 per month." It's true! There's no need to doubt or hold back. Instead, let's celebrate this success in advance. Using gestures can be a simple yet powerful tool to help reset your internal compass and develop new neurological pathways for success. By observing successful and happy individuals and mimicking their body language, you can actually change your own internal representation and achieve the same level of success and happiness."

Chapter 5, Assignment

Note: Please write your answers or actions in the space provided after each task and make full use of it.

What is your physiology when you are upset or sad?

___

___

___

___

___

___

___

___

___

___

What is your physiological state when you feel happy and accomplished?

____

____

____

____

____

____

____

____

____

____

____

____

Rember happy memories, write down and set your mindset by recalling powerful memories from your past.

____

____

Choose a single impactful gesture with the intention of creating a state of resourcefulness through the "AS IF" technique.

____

____

____

____

____

____

____

____

____

____

Practice and perform that specific gesture while reciting the affirmations provided. Infuse it with enthusiasm. Speak out loud and truly feel its empowering effect. Write your experiences.

____

____

CHAPTER 6, SECRET #5

"Write it down. Written goals have a way of transforming wishes into wants; cant's into cans; dreams into plans; and plans into reality. Don't just think it – INK IT!"

Micheal Korda

We often have many desires in our minds, wanting to achieve various things and become someone in life. These aspirations tend to change over time, just like how a child's desires can fluctuate from day to day. One moment, they want to be a pilot, and the next, a doctor. It's human nature to crave having, being, and doing everything in life.

Having desires in life is important, but what matters most is achieving them within a specific timeframe. Research shows that only 33 percent of people have clear goals, and among those, only 33 percent actually think and talk about their goals.

This means that just 10.89 percent of people actively remind themselves of their goals, and out of that group, only 33 percent write their goals down. In other words, a mere 3.59 percent of people commit their goals to writing. And out of that 3.59 percent, just 1.18 percent regularly review their written goals. Now, if we consider the overall population, how many people can truly be called successful? How many billionaires are there in the world? A quick Google search will confirm these percentages.

According to a report from Suisse (TRT World), there are 52 million people in the top-tier one percent, and all of them are millionaires. Among this exclusive group, there are 175,000 ultra-wealthy individuals, which represents 0.1 percent of the total. These individuals collectively possess 25 percent of the world's wealth. Therefore, can we infer that the remaining 75 percent of the world's wealth is owned by 99.9 percent of people? What does this imply? It suggests that "Successful

People" are not simply born; they can be developed.

If you aspire to achieve success and accumulate billions of rupees while maintaining perfect health and happiness in your relationships, it is crucial to begin documenting the affirmations you have developed thus far. By writing them down, you will gain a clearer comprehension of their meaning.

"Goals that are not written down are just wishes."

– Fitzhugh Dodson

Why are written goals important? What is the science behind them? I'm sure these questions are on your mind. Let's delve into the science behind it.

Once you have a clear understanding of what you want and can create accurate affirmations, it is essential to write them down. Writing affirmations is an action performed by the subconscious mind, allowing for the development of new neural pathways. By writing affirmations, we can quickly register them in our subconscious mind. This process is similar to the experience of writing and remembering information during our school years, where we often found that writing things down helped us retain them better than simply listening to lectures or reading theory. When we write our desires or goal statements as affirmations, our mind becomes fully engaged in the process, which accelerates the manifestation of our desired goals. By giving attention to our desires through writing, we can achieve our goals more rapidly.

The Science of Writing Goals.

Writing affirmations is a powerful tool for clearing away vague or unclear thoughts. By creating affirmations, we can bring clarity and consistency to our thinking, eliminating any clouded or unwanted ideas. This practice also helps us to distinguish between what we truly want and what we don't want in our lives. To harness the full potential of affirmations, start by deciding what you want and crafting affirmations using the techniques outlined in this book. Then, combine the secret numbers 2, 3, 4, and 5 to amplify the impact of your affirmations. By following these steps, you will unlock the power to create miracles in your life.

When I created affirmations for myself and wrote them down, I felt a great sense of happiness knowing that they would soon become reality. However, I made the mistake of keeping my written affirmations in a drawer and forgetting about them. I went on vacation for a few days, and upon returning home, I struggled to remember my affirmations, desires, and dreams. It was surprising to me how I had almost completely forgotten what I had written about my goals, and my thoughts about my desires became unclear. My mind started generating new ideas, tempting me to create new goals based on these exciting thoughts.

All the goals I had previously set and written down seemed to have vanished. But when I opened my goal diary again to write new goals, seeing my previous goals reminded me of my purpose. It helped me recall my intentions and made me realize that writing goals once is not enough; it is equally important to reread and remember them multiple times a day. Since then, I have made it a habit to carry my goal diary with me. Whenever I have a moment, I open it and read my written affirmations. This simple act serves as a reminder of my life purpose, helps me achieve my goals more quickly, and keeps me focused.

After writing your goals as affirmations, it is important to regularly reread and remind yourself of them throughout the day.

"Clear written goals have a wonderful effect on your thinking, they motivate you and galvanize them into action. They stimulate your creativity, release your energy, and help you to overcome

procrastination as much as any other factor."

Brain Tracy

Power of Reviewing

Once you have written your goals, make sure to regularly remind yourself of them by reading them throughout the day. It is also important to periodically review your goals. If you have set goals with specific deadlines and find that you are unable to achieve them within that timeframe, you can adjust the time or action plans as needed.

Regularly reviewing written goals is the most crucial task. It acts as a milestone, providing direction and guidance, ensuring that our desired outcomes remain on track. Unfortunately, many people neglect this vital step, leading to a frequent inability to achieve their goals. It's important to note that while the goals themselves should remain unchanged, the action plan can be modified through regular review. We have the power to adjust our action plans, but not our goals. So, adopt the manifestation formula:

Manifest Goals = Write the Goals + Read the Goals Daily + Review them time to time

When Olympic decathlon gold medalist Burce Jenner asked a roomful of Olympic hopefuls if they had a list of written goals, every one raised their hands. When he asked how many of them had that list with them right that moment, only one person raised his hand. That person was Dan O'Brien. And it was Dan O'Brien who went on to win the gold medal in the Decathlon at the 1996 Olympics in Atlanta. Don't underestimate the power of setting goals and constantly reviewing them. – Jack Canfield

Chapter 6, Assignment

Note: Please write your answers or actions in the space provided after each task and make full use of it.

Establish clear goal statements for Health in your life.

____

____

____

____

____

Establish clear goal statements for Wealth in your life.

____

____

____

____

Establish clear goal statements for Relationships in your life.

____

____

____

____

____

____

Establish clear goal statements for career in your life.

____

____

____

____

____

____

Read your affirmations twice a day and write your experiences here.

____

____

____

____

____

____

____

____

____

____

____

____

CHAPTER 7, SECRET #6

"Meditation will change your life for the better, enhance your physical health, improve your sleep, and help you achieve your goals, both material and spiritual."

Deepak Chopra

The earliest records of meditation (Dhyana) can be traced back to the ancient Hindus' holy book called the "Vedas." Since the 19th century, meditation has spread to various cultures, and it is now mentioned in every country, religion, and holy book. Meditation is considered to be the ancient art of living and is seen as the proper way of life for humans. In the 1960s, Paul MacLean introduced the concept of the triune brain, which proposes that we have one mind and three brains.

1. Reptilian Brain
2. Emotional Brain
3. Rational Brain

Reptilian brain

The reptilian brain, which first appeared in fish and is 500 million years older, is located in the brainstem. It is responsible for controlling vital bodily functions such as heart rate, breathing, body temperature, and balance. Its primary goal is survival and it is constantly seeking safety. The reptilian brain communicates through body sensations and impulses, and it triggers instinctive responses.

Emotional Brain

It is almost 150 million years old and originally developed in small mammals. This incredible ability is known as emotions. Emotions enable us to remember behaviors that result in pleasant or unpleasant experiences. The human brain, the center for our value judgments, plays a significant role in our behavior, often without our awareness. It possesses emotional states and can experience the powerful emotion of love. Furthermore, it comprehends the language of emotions and understands various feeling tones. It also has emotional experiences and implicit memory.

Rational Brain

The brain is believed to be between 2 to 3 million years old. It became increasingly significant in primates and reached its peak in the human brain, which is characterized by two large cerebral hemispheres that play a central role. These hemispheres are responsible for the evolution of human language, abstract thinking, imagination, and consciousness. The Rational Brain, as it is commonly referred to, is highly adaptable and capable of infinite learning. It is also the driving force behind the development of human cultures. The Rational Brain operates in an execution state and is constantly in search of new knowledge. It primarily comprehends and expresses thoughts and ideas through language.

It is fascinating to note that the three parts of the brain do not function in isolation; rather, they are interconnected. When the Reptilian brain detects a threat through physical sensations, the Emotional brain responds by generating fearful or stressful emotions and relaying signals to the Rational brain. The Rational brain, equipped with freewill, vast potential, and the ability to learn and carry out behaviors, then employs logic to find creative ways to protect individuals. It possesses the capacity to achieve desired outcomes through conscious efforts, self-awareness, and deliberate thought.

MEDITATION - A BRIDGE

Our mind operates automatically in response to different situations. The three parts of the brain work together to produce the intended outcomes. However, there are instances when our emotional brain holds onto painful memories and fails to communicate effectively with the reptilian and rational brain. In such cases, meditation serves as a conscious practice that can bring awareness to these trapped emotions and facilitate the integration of all three brain functions.

Meditation practice serves to connect all three aspects - our emotions, thoughts, and inner peace. Daily meditation is essential if you seek desired results in life, as it brings a multitude of benefits. Consider meditation as a form of medication, as it promotes emotional, physical, and mental well-being while offering clarity of thought and the creation of new neurological pathways.

We are unable to swim in a storm, much like how we cannot achieve our goals with unclear thoughts and emotions. A clear and peaceful mind is the key to attaining everything we desire in life. Dedicate 20 minutes each day to practicing meditation, allowing yourself to sweep away any inner clutter. Empty your mind and cleanse it daily.

Meditation techniques vary across different cultures and religions. However, I would like to recommend to you an ancient meditation practice called "Anapana Sati," which was taught by Gautam Buddha thousands of years ago. In this guide, you will learn the step-by-step process of practicing "Anapana Sati" meditation.

Close your eyes, sit in a straight and comfortable position, and simply observe your natural and gentle breath.

Avoid any breathing exercises and instead, just observe your breath. Notice whether your breath is shallow or deep, fast or slow.

To achieve relaxation, simply begin by observing your breath. As you watch your breath, both your conscious and rational mind will naturally relax.

By watching your breath, you can consciously bring your focus to the present moment. As a result, the frequency of thoughts will gradually be reduced. This stage is known as the "Dhyana" stage.

Meditation involves being fully present in the moment, and the act of breathing serves as the primary tool to help us achieve this state. You may be wondering why it is so crucial to be in the present moment, and this is an excellent question. Let's delve into the scientific explanation behind the significance of being fully present.

POWER IS IN THE PRESENT MOMENT

Humans tend to constantly think about their past or future, whether consciously or unconsciously. We often find ourselves worrying about what lies ahead or dwelling on past events. Rarely do we truly live in the present moment. However, through meditation, we can deliberately shift our attention to the here and now by observing our natural and gentle breath. The present moment is where life exists. It is where power resides. In fact, it is in the present moment that we have the ability to shape our future. Dwelling in the past or future will not bring us the desired outcomes we seek. By focusing on our breath and embracing the present moment, we unlock the connections between different parts of our brain.

The rational brain has the ability to consciously observe all bodily sensations and emotions stored in the emotional brain. By creating conscious awareness of these sensations and emotions, it provides the wisdom to perceive them as an impartial observer. The key is to simply observe without reacting, allowing all emotions and sensations to naturally fade away. This practice is known as "Vipassana" sadhna. To fully learn this practice, it is necessary to attend a 10-day residential camp where you can experience the process in-depth. However, for now, you can begin with "Anapana Sati" meditation, which will help you manifest desired results in your life.

I am sharing the script of a meditation aimed at helping you achieve your goals. You can read this script, record it in your own voice, and then begin practicing it. This meditation is referred to as secret #6.

Meditation Script to Manifest Goals

Gently close your eyes and as you do, give a beautiful smile and simply relax. Pay attention to your breath and remember, there is no need to do "Pranayama" or any other breathing exercises.

Just observe your natural, gentle breath for a few moments. Take a brief pause and watch your breath for about 2 seconds. I understand that it may be challenging to observe the breath continuously. Therefore, I will now guide you through a simple technique to help you watch your breath more easily.

Direct your attention to your upper lip, where you will be inhaling and exhaling. Remain focused on this area for the next 5 seconds. Watch the breath..... Simply, just watch the breath... Do it for 5 seconds more....

Still, you may have lingering thoughts on your mind. However, there is no need to worry. It is important to not suppress or disregard them.Your only job is to focus on your breath.....natural, tender breath.....

Wonderful...

You are making considerable progress and steadily enhancing your skills. You can gradually intensify your focus on your breath. And you can now observe that the frequency of your thoughts has decreased....

Wonderful, dear learner....

Where can one find the essence of life? Life resides within the present moment, as this moment represents the ultimate truth for each individual. Embrace it fully, allowing yourself to connect with your breath and derive enjoyment from the entirety of this experiential process.

Wonderful...

Once you have achieved a state of complete relaxation and can maintain focus on your breathfor an extended period, it is time to embark on the process of revitalizing your life through the power of affirmations. Whether spoken aloud or silently within your mind, allow yourself to fully construct new neural pathways. When you feel prepared, commence the practice of affirming your intentions.

For Example,

1. I am ***amazed*** & grateful to have perfect health.
2. I ***feel fantastic*** & grateful to earn $ 10,000 per month consistently and regularly.
3. I am so **happy** & grateful to have wonderful relationships with my parents.
4. I ***feel supportive*** and I am grateful to have very supportive people at my workplace.

Repeat each exercise 10 times. Once you have completed the repetitions, gently rub your palms together and place them over your closed eyes. Slowly open your eyes while maintaining the warmth of your palms on your face. Finally, remove your palms from your face and return to a relaxed state.

Welcome back....

The aforementioned script is designed to assist in the realization of one's goals. When utilizing the script for personal purposes, it is advisable to substitute the pronouns "YOU" and "YOUR" with "I" and "MY" respectively. Additionally, there is the possibility to incorporate additional affirmations. The individual has the freedom to concentrate on a particular area or affirm in all areas as desired. It is important to emphasize that the decision lies solely with the individual. It is recommended to engage in 10 minutes of daily meditation alongside the utilization of this script in order to effectively manifest the desired outcomes.

Happy meditating!

CHAPTER 7, ASSIGNMENT

Note: Please write your answers or actions in the space provided after each task and make full use of it.

Ensure that you document your affirmations in area of Health.

Ensure that you document your affirmations in area of Wealth.

Ensure that you document your affirmations in area of Relationships.

____

____

____

____

____

____

____

____

____

____

____

____

Ensure that you document your affirmations in area of Career.

Establish and cultivate your gestures in conjunction with affirmations.

____

____

____

____

____

____

____

Now, please locate a suitable and relaxing environment for the next 15 minutes in order to engage in the meditation practice, utilizing the "Meditation script to Manifest your goals."

CHAPTER 8, SECRET #7

"If you want to reach a goal, you must see reaching in your mind before you actually arrive at your goal."

Zig Ziglar

A baby starts learning from pictures. Do you remember your preschool books? They're full of pictures. We have been shown different pictures and told their names, and we, being a baby, learned easily through pictures' language. Initially, a baby cannot identify spellings or letters but can easily identify the pictures. Babies memorize and decode names and spellings through pictures. Pictures help the human mind to identify the object or help to understand any information easily and effectively.

The human mind possesses a variety of methods for comprehending information, and the utilization of visual aids, such as pictures, stands out as one of the most potent and accessible tools. Unlike the conscious mind, the subconscious mind lacks logical faculties and cannot engage in independent thinking or decision-making. Rather, it functions by processing the available information, with the acquisition of new knowledge facilitated effortlessly through visual stimuli. Consequently, a significant portion of our accumulated knowledge exists in pictorial form within our minds. For instance, upon closing your eyes and envisioning an elephant, your mind promptly conjures an image of said animal. Due to our early exposure to and subsequent learning of the visual representation of an elephant, it becomes impossible for our minds to generate images of a horse or a dog.

5 Senses

The human body continuously receives information through the senses of sight (visual), sound (auditory), smell (olfactory), taste (gustatory), and touch (kinesthetic), and transmits it to our subconscious mind. Our mind consistently processes information from what we see, hear, taste, smell, and touch, with visual stimuli being particularly impactful compared to other sensory inputs. This is why we are all drawn to watching movies or videos, as our minds readily absorb information through visual means. Research also indicates that 65 percent of people are visual learners. Understanding the immense power of the subconscious mind, let us now consciously utilize it to manifest our desired goals.

The Visualization Technique

Please close your eyes and envision your goals as if you have successfully accomplished them. This is the most effective means of manifesting your aspirations.

"When you visualize, then you materialize."

Denis Waitly

Please ensure that you visualize everything with utmost clarity and attention to detail. The more precise your visualization is, the more effectively you will be able to conceptualize your desired outcome.

Create a mental film - a mental film depicting your own life. Shape your future in the present moment using visualization techniques.

Visualize with HD clarity, incorporating intricate details as though you were envisioning your very own abode. Now, gently shut your eyes and embark upon a mental journey, vividly picturing your ideal sanctuary within your mind's eye.

Visualize the appearance of the residence, including its architecture, color scheme, interior design, and entrance.

Please proceed to enter your residence and thoroughly examine each area. Observe the hue of the walls, inspect the kitchen, and evaluate the furniture. Take note of the texture of the furnishings and envision the color scheme of the curtains, as well as the dimensions of the windows. Lastly, venture out onto the bedroom balcony, as well as explore the backyard and garden of your property.

Visualize the momentous occasion when you are handed the key to your long-awaited dream home. Immerse yourself in the emotions that accompany this joyous event and express your sincere gratitude. Allow yourself to fully experience the feelings of happiness and contentment that arise. Treat this visualization exercise as if you were taking a personal virtual tour of your dream home - a cherished activity that is to be repeated daily for a duration of 10 minutes.

The visualization process knows no limits. You have the freedom to visualize anything your heart desires. If you possess the ability to visualize, you have the power to manifest. The cost of visualization is of no concern, and there is no need for a visa to embark on a virtual tour. There are no bills to be paid in order to watch your mental movie. It is your realm, and through visualization, you can shape it. Regardless of your background, origin, qualifications, communication abilities, skin color, gender, religion, or nationality, you have the ability to create a future from any corner of the world.

Your subconscious mind brings forth your desires by means of visualization. Each individual possesses inherent gifts and is influenced by the power of the subconscious mind, thereby possessing the capacity to engage in visualization.

Primary Words

Many individuals often claim that they lack visual aptitude and struggle with visualization.

To immerse yourself and engage your mind, close your eyes and visualize your kitchen. Now, go to your kitchen and find the refrigerator. Open the door, grab a water bottle, and then close the door tightly. Return to your seat and savor the refreshing drink.

Can you do it? Have you taken a look at your kitchen? Have you examined your refrigerator? If so, then you possess the ability to visualize. The human mind is inherently capable of comprehending visual language. Now, attempt the same exercise once more for a different scenario.

Close your eyes and imagine your favorite natural place, where you can see a magnificent banyan tree.

Imagine yourself standing right in front of a magnificent banyan tree. Now, focus your attention on the tree itself, rather than the white horse that is happily munching on grass beneath it.

Now, open your eyes and describe what you have observed. You would notice a serene natural setting, a majestic banyan tree, and a graceful white horse peacefully grazing on grass. This demonstrates that our subconscious mind does not comprehend words like "No, Not, Don't, Won't". Instead, it selects the primary word from the sentence and presents it to you on your mental screen. You can experiment with other objects to gain a deeper understanding of this phenomenon. It will be an enjoyable exercise.

STEPS TO VISUALIZATION

- Now that you possess powerful tools to manifest your goals, it is time to integrate them and begin using them collectively.
- Write down all of your goals in the form of affirmations, utilizing Secret #1.
- Harness the power of "Gratitude" and incorporate it into your affirmation using secret #2.
- Now, take a moment to meditate for 10 minutes using secret #6.
- Keep meditating and, while in this meditative position, begin visualizing your

goals. Take one goal at a time and visualize it in great detail and with utmost precision. Imagine in your mind a vivid and detailed movie of your goals. Envision yourself already having achieved what you desire in life. Secret #7.

- Experience the emotions of excitement, joy, and happiness while visualizing. This is a crucial step in the manifestation process. If you approach each step as a ritual but fail to truly feel the entire process during visualization, your goals may not be realized. Allow yourself to feel the joy of accomplishing your objectives. Celebrate your successes with gratitude, and you will effortlessly attain your desires. Apply secret #3.
- Once you have finished visualizing, open your eyes and begin writing your goals in your journal or on the computer, utilizing secret #5.

- Finish your writing, and now is the perfect time to demonstrate the gesture of success, the gesture of achievement.
- Stand up and raise your hand for each goal. If possible, speak your affirmation out loud or say it silently in your mind while performing a corresponding gesture. Employ secret #4.

You can customize your approach. Begin by writing affirmations, then perform the fire gesture, followed by meditation and visualization. The important thing is to utilize all the secrets in unison. It won't be effective if you write affirmations today, meditate on them tomorrow, and visualize them on a different day. Think of it as a recipe. All the ingredients are needed to create a delicious dish. If one ingredient is missing, the dish won't be enjoyable. Similarly, to easily achieve results in life, you must use all seven secrets together. This harnesses the power of your subconscious mind and its familiar language.

Practicing all seven secrets simultaneously helps you quickly create new mental territory.

All successful people, whether they are aware of it or not, employ these secrets. Now, it is your turn. You have already learned seven secrets. Begin implementing them collectively and reach your desired goals.

Chapter 8, Assignment

Note: Please write your answers or actions in the space provided after each task and make full use of it.

Choose a single goal and commit to practicing visualization every day for the next 21 days.

Day 1, ____________________________________

____

Day 2 :____________________________________

____

Day 3, ____________________________________

____

Day 4 :____________________________________

____

Day 5, ____________________________________

____

Day 6 :____________________________________

____

Day 7, ____

____

Day 9 :____

____

Day 10, _______________________________________

____

Day 11 :_______________________________________

____

Day 12, _______________________________________

____

Day 13 :_______________________________________

____

Day 14, _______________________________________

____

Day 15 :______________________________

____

Day 16, ______________________________

____

Day 17 :______________________________

____

Day 18, ______________________________

____

Day 19 :______________________________

____

Day 20, ______________________________

____

Day 21 :______________________________

Follow these seven steps every day to manifest the goals you desire in life and write down your everyday experiences here

Day 1, ________________________________

Day 2 :________________________________

Day 3, ________________________________

Day 4 :________________________________

Day 5, ________________________________

Day 6 :________________________________

Day 7, ________________________________

Day 9 :________________________________

Day 10, ________________________________

Day 11 :________________________________

Day 12, ________________________________

Day 13 :________________________________

Day 14, ________________________________

Day 15 :______________________________

Day 16, ______________________________

Day 17 :______________________________

Day 18, ______________________________

Day 19 :______________________________

Day 20, ______________________________

Day 21 :______________________________

Chapter 9, Secret#8

"When you dance to your own RHYTHM, Life taps its toes to your beat."

"Terry Guillemets"

The universe operates on rhythmic systems. Each planet has its own place, and even everything on Earth follows a rhythm. The Sun rises, the Moon undergoes daily shape changes, water flows, oceans wave, flowers bloom, birds chirp, seeds grow into saplings and saplings grow into trees that bear fruit. Water evaporates and becomes clouds in the sky, rain falls at the right time, and every species on this planet has its own unique rhythm. Nature functions in perfect synchronization, creating a harmonious rhythm. It is like a beautiful melody. Have you ever taken the time to listen to the music of chirping birds, the wind rustling through the trees, clouds gently brushing against mountains, or water flowing in a spring? Have you ever noticed the rhythm of life beneath the ocean's surface?

Silence possesses its own inherent rhythm.

In our journey through life, we transition from being fetuses to becoming adults. Our heart tirelessly beats and pumps blood throughout our entire body, while our kidneys diligently purify the blood and eliminate toxins through urine. Oxygenated blood circulates, providing ample oxygen to nourish our organs. The stomach diligently digests the food we consume, and waste is excreted after proper assimilation. Every aspect of our body, from organs to cells and tissues, is interconnected and operates in flawless harmony. Life thrives in every corner, and the rhythm of life is ever-present.

Have you ever seen a baby in a cradle, who doesn't know any language and can't even speak, but still loves his mother's lullaby? The mother's lullaby is filled with rhymes and rhythm, which the child enjoys. It's amazing how the child stops crying and falls asleep when hearing the lullaby. The child recognizes his mother's voice, catches onto the tune of the lullaby, and finds joy in the rhymes and rhythms. But what does it all mean? Why is the child able to relax so quickly, even though he doesn't understand a single word? Let's dive into the science behind it.

Technique to Use the Rhymes and Rhythms

We are inherently connected to nature. In fact, we are nature. Nature operates in rhythms, and as humans, we are naturally drawn to rhythms as well. It is important to grasp this scientific concept and intentionally apply it in order to achieve the desired outcomes in your life.

Choose one affirmation and select your favorite song, which can be any song from a movie or an album by your favorite singer.

Now, select the melody of that song and substitute the lyrics with your own affirming sentences.

Create your own song, one that resonates with your mind, a song that already brings you joy and has a positive neurological association. Choose a song that always brings you enjoyment and helps uplift your mood, a song that makes you want to dance. Select a rhythm for your song and incorporate your affirmation as lyrics.

If possible, please add the karaoke for the song. There are numerous online karaoke or mobile applications that you can use. Feel free to be creative with your song, incorporating new sounds and music as you see fit. This is your opportunity to truly express yourself and share your life through music. Sing it beautifully and fully enjoy the experience. Sing the song all day long and if you desire, you can even record your own voice and listen to it daily.

When you embrace the law of rhythms, your mind naturally becomes receptive to all commands. Adding a joyful gesture while singing your life song enhances the results. Your mind is already familiar with the melody you have chosen.

Here, we tap into the power of our subconscious mind. Our minds are filled with vast amounts of information, which we use without even realizing it. Our subconscious mind acts as a reference, guiding our actions without our conscious awareness.

Use of "Happy Neurological Path"

For instance, recalling a natural place immediately induces relaxation in our minds. Why does this happen? It is because we have all personally witnessed the splendor of nature. We have experienced the serenity and tranquility found in these natural settings. Our minds have the ability to retain emotions, and these emotions activate positive neural pathways associated with nature, subsequently transmitting signals of peace and calmness to our subconscious minds.

Now, close your eyes and tap into the wisdom of your subconscious mind. Take a moment to reflect and observe what unfolds. Did you feel a sense of relaxation as you recalled the serene natural setting? Chances are, your answer is "Yes." Your mind is drawing upon a blissful neural pathway, where it has previously experienced tranquility and serenity. It is now reflecting that same sense of calmness and peace in the present moment.

We are now consciously harnessing the power of the same science. By tapping into existing neurological pathways, we can relive the joyous experiences stored in our minds. Throughout our lives, we have accumulated a repertoire of songs. From the tender lullabies our mothers sang to us, to the playful rhymes of our kindergarten days, to the poetry and melodies that accompanied us through school and university. These songs hold a special place in our minds, instantly capturing our attention. Now that we understand their ability to activate positive neurological pathways, we can leverage this knowledge to achieve our desired outcomes. Embrace this scientific approach and unlock unlimited possibilities in your life.

In secret #8, we are utilizing the existing neurological pathways instead of creating new ones to achieve our goals.

Now, you are ready to utilize the well-established neurological pathways. The process is quite simple - select your favorite song, substitute the lyrics with your affirmation, and if feasible, sing it with karaoke.

Don't worry about the quality of your voice or tone, or how well you sing. Just focus on singing and enjoying your song. Remember, it is your life's song, and you are the one in charge of redesigning your life. No one else can do that for you. So go ahead, sing it, dance it, and most importantly, enjoy it.

Make time throughout the day to sing your song. It doesn't matter if you're driving, biking, waiting in line, walking in the garden, or in the kitchen; just sing and dance to it, and enjoy yourself. By doing this, your mind will receive positive and happy signals. It will start to believe in what you affirm, and this will make it easier and more joyful for you to manifest whatever you want in your life.

For example,

My song is by Celine Dion is,"I get wings to fly...Oh oh I am alive......When you call on me, when I hear you breathe...I get wings to fly....I feel that I am alive...." Now, I utilize the rhythms of the song and substitute its lyrics with my own affirmations. I sing and derive daily enjoyment from them.

What song is your favorite?

Chapter 9, Assignment

Note: Please write your answers or actions in the space provided after each task and make full use of it.

Choose your favorite song and write the lyrics of it.

Replace the lyrics with your own affirmations and compose a new song.

- Maintain the same rhythm and, if possible, incorporate karaoke or mix in different music.
- Sing your song and fully embrace the emotions it carries.
- Dance, enjoy, and fully embrace the feeling.
- To achieve your desired goal in life, record and sing your song daily.

Write down your experiences by applying secret #8

____

____

____

____

____

____

____

____

Chapter 10, Secret #9

"Love only grows by sharing. You can only have more for yourself by giving it away to others."

-Brain Tracy

Once upon a time, there lived a farmer who grew high quality award-winning corn. Each year he would participate in the state farmer's fair and win the gold medal for his exceptionally good corns.

The farmer's high-quality corn was praised all around in the state. The success story of exceptional corn reached to the ears of the journalist and he wanted to interview the farmer. While he was learning about the agriculture process of the farmer, he discovered that the farmer shared his best quality seeds with his neighbors.

"How can you afford to share your best corn seeds with your neighbors when some of them compete with you in the agriculture fair?", asked the curious reporter.

"Why wouldn't I, sir?", asked the farmer. Didn't you know that wind picks up pollen from the ripening corn and swirls it from the field to field. If my neighbors grow inferior quality corn, cross pollination would eventually degrade the quality of my corn too. If I am to grow high-quality corn, I must help my neighbors grow a good corn too!"

"To achieve success, help others grow." This principle is inherent in nature. What we give to the world, we receive in return. The universe mirrors our thoughts and actions. This well-known story illustrates how success can be attained by sharing and caring for others as they pursue their own path to success.

From an early age, we are often taught not to share. Parents commonly instruct their children to withhold notes or study tips from their classmates, saying things like "Don't share your tiffin," "Don't share your ideas," or "Don't share your gazettes," and so on. While children may have a natural inclination to share their belongings with friends, they are prevented from doing so. The act of sharing has been discouraged since childhood.

WHY DON'T WE SHARE?

Generally, people often refrain from sharing their belongings or ideas with others due to fear. This fear is often rooted in the fear of failure.

The fear of failure does not contribute to success. In life, you always have the option to grow, but fear hinders that growth.

Two friends, who had grown up together and completed their university studies, found themselves working at the same company. After a few years, one friend was promoted to a managerial position within the company, while the other friend had not yet received a promotion.

The first friend's success can be attributed to his willingness to help others in the office. He consistently went above and beyond to support the growth of his colleagues, sharing his knowledge with them. He was fearless and didn't believe in competition. Throughout his journey of unknowingly contributing to others' lives, he developed his own leadership potential.

On the other hand, the second friend was always secretive about his knowledge. He would continuously criticize others in order to showcase his own abilities to the management. His belief was that by putting others down through criticism, he would automatically be recognized for his own potential. Unfortunately, he never made an effort to improve his own skills and was constantly focused on demotivating others. As a result, he ultimately failed in his workplace. He neither developed himself nor utilized his knowledge to benefit the company.

When you are filled with fear and reluctant to share anything with others, you attract more situations that trigger fear into your life. Fear is a detrimental emotion, and negative emotions never yield positive outcomes in life.

I don't believe that you should share all of your personal life or office secrets with others at the workplace. I also don't believe that we should share everything with everyone all the time. However, I do strongly recommend that you assist others as much as you can, while keeping official and personal secrets confidential.

There are often moments when we have the chance to assist others without dedicating a significant amount of time or effort. However, if we allow ourselves to feel insecure and fear competition, we miss out on these opportunities to lend a hand.

Fear hinders personal growth and development in life.

If you have the ability to grow in life and the drive to develop your own potential, you have no reason to fear competition. Lack of self-confidence hinders collaboration, and criticizing others only reveals one's own lack of confidence.

Everyone is a unique individual, and there is no one quite like them. Each person is on their own unique journey, equipped with specific skill sets and time constraints. Our purpose is to learn from one another and grow individually. Therefore, let us foster a culture of collaboration, eradicate the fear of failure from our minds, and extend our assistance to others as much as we can.

SCIENCE BEHIND SHARING

When you contribute your time, knowledge, money, skills, or infrastructure to others, you are demonstrating to your subconscious mind that you are valuable, capable, and have a lot to offer the world. You have the potential to achieve, become, and possess anything in life. Helping others is a beautiful act that, without us even realizing it, communicates feelings of worthiness to our subconscious mind.

All religions advocate for sharing, and gurus provide us with the chance to assist those in need within our communities. Numerous non-governmental organizations dedicate their efforts to improve society in various ways, including education, healthcare, relationships, careers, and environmental preservation. These groups tirelessly work towards the betterment of our society and nation as a whole. In our daily lives, we all rely on the support and services of others, often without even realizing it.

This teaches us that as we grow, we should make a conscious effort to uplift others, just as we have been uplifted, whether knowingly or unknowingly. By lifting others, we ourselves reach the top. And by continuing to help others throughout our lives, we will remain at the top.

You will experience personal growth by helping others. Your mind will clearly understand that you have the ability to provide information, spend money or time, teach, offer infrastructure, and more. When your subconscious mind receives these signals of capability, it will begin to act accordingly. It's as simple as that!

Now, apply the same scientific principles intentionally to manifest the desired outcomes in your life. Begin by expressing what you desire in your life. What is it that you want? Do you desire financial abundance? Then actively share your wealth. Do you seek happiness in a relationship? Then cultivate and share love and joy within your relationships. Do you long for optimal health? Then engage in activities that promote wellness, surround yourself with healthy individuals, and adopt their healthy lifestyle. By doing so, you will attain the very things you desire.

How can someone share money when they don't have enough in their pocket? How can someone offer love in a relationship when they are feeling sad or financially depleted? How can a person promote health when they themselves are unhealthy? The only answer I have for all of these questions is "Like attracts like!"

I'm not suggesting that you borrow money and help others just to make yourself feel good and expect financial gain. I don't advocate for false happiness and health in the world. My intention is to guide you in making the most of the resources you have. I would like to share a widely accepted message on this topic.

"When God blesses you financially, Don't raise your standard of living. Raise your standard of giving."

"No one has ever become poor by giving."

Anne Frank

10% Principle

If you have $100, set aside 10 percent of it as a separate fund for charity. You can use this fund to buy clothes for the poor, provide food, offer shelter, pay medical bills, or cover education fees. There are numerous ways you can help others with your 10 percent charity fund. It's time to decide how you would like to contribute to society.

We possess a conditional mindset. We express a desire to make a contribution to society, but only under the condition that, someday in the future, when I have amassed immense wealth, I will extend assistance to others. Someday, when my relationships are filled with happiness, then I will show respect towards people. Someday, when I am in a state of good health, then I will actively promote well-being. However, this hypothetical situation will never come to pass. When we think and speak in this manner, we effectively communicate to our subconscious mind that we are currently lacking in wealth, happiness, and health. Consequently, our subconscious mind begins to mirror these beliefs. It is important to note that someday will never materialize.

To create a bright future, it is important to focus on giving and helping others in the present moment. It is impossible to create a future while being stuck in the future itself. Instead, you have the power to shape your future by taking action in the present moment. Start by recognizing your conditioned thinking patterns and work on unlocking them. These conditions often act as barriers to your success.

When I obtained employment, the salary and job held great significance for me due to my familial obligations. Every single penny of my salary carried weight. However, upon receiving my first paycheck, I allocated 60% of it towards purchasing a pricey mobile phone for my father.

I did not receive love and respect from my parents and brother. However, when I adopted two children, I wholeheartedly dedicated myself to them as their non-biological mother. I raised them with love and affection, providing them with everything I had ever wanted in life.

I had a strong desire to heal my life and overcome the challenges I faced. For many years, I experienced sadness and frustration in my relationship. To address these issues, I attended personal development seminars, read books, pursued various courses, and even began teaching others the same modalities and wisdom. And the amazing result? I now enjoy financial freedom, happiness in my relationships with my parents, spouse, children, and myself, perfect health, and ongoing spiritual growth.

The secret to success is "sharing." When you start sharing what you have, you will receive it back multiplied thousands of times. I have numerous examples from my own life. For instance, when I gifted a costly mobile phone to my father, I didn't expect anything in return. When I show love to my children, I don't expect anything in return. When I teach valuable, priceless, and life-changing lessons to people through my YouTube channel, I also don't expect anything in return. However, I must mention that an unknown source consistently aids me in all aspects of my life. I am always divinely guided, loved, and respected. Money flows to me easily and effortlessly. I find solutions to every problem swiftly. My children are thriving in their lives, and my husband is achieving great success in his business. What more could I ask for from the universe?

I am delighted to be able to contribute my love and wisdom to humanity. Sharing is like the final touch that enhances everything. Once you have learned all eight secrets, your foundation is ready. Now, it's time to add that final touch. Begin sharing what you have with others. By embracing the act of "sharing" and making a conscious effort to do it regularly, without any expectations in return, your whole life will be transformed. This transformation will encompass your health, wealth, relationships, spirituality, and career, leading to success in all these areas.

Believe me, you will never experience a shortage of money in your life. You will always find happiness with your loved ones and thrive in your career. Have you ever encountered someone who contributes to society and yet is unhappy or unhealthy? The answer is a resounding "NO!"

One day, a boy visited Guruji multiple times to receive "Prasad." Each time he received it, he promptly shared it with others. A volunteer at the ashram observed this and suggested to Guruji that he should stop giving "Prasad" to the boy, as it was intended to be given only once a day to one person. Guruji, however, smiled and responded that he would continue to give "Prasad" to the boy as long as he continued to share it with others. Guruji conveyed that his blessings, in the form of "Prasad," were always available to those who were willing to lovingly share it unconditionally.

You would receive it from an unknown source. If you selflessly help others without expecting anything in return, you will experience rapid personal growth. This is a fundamental law of nature. Nature always gives to us unconditionally, without expecting anything in return. We are not separate from nature; we are its children and an integral part of it. Therefore, helping others is inherent to our nature. Remind yourself daily of the importance of making a positive impact on others' lives. Our mind recognizes that honorable individuals are those who assist others. By demonstrating this through sharing, you are affirming to your mind that you are worthy, and as a result, your mind will manifest the same positive outcomes.

When we help others, we become the richest people in the world. It doesn't matter if our contribution is small, whether it's monetary or any other form of assistance; what matters is that we do it sincerely. Help others without any conditions. Do it consistently. Humans have countless desires and dreams, and they never truly cease. As soon as we fulfill one, another takes its place, drawing us towards it and prompting us to pursue it. The list of wishes and desires is endless. It's a natural part of life to pursue our dreams one after another, but it's equally important to help others along the way. Sharing is a way of life. We should never wait until we are old or until we become billionaires to start sharing. You become a billionaire as soon as you start helping others. We don't need millions of dollars to assist others, and always remember that when we help others, we are actually helping ourselves first! Happy Sharing!

Chapter 10, Assignment

Note: Please write your answers or actions in the space provided after each task and make full use of it.

Set aside 10 percent of your income each month and use it to support others by providing clothing, housing, medical expenses, education fees, food, sharing your skills, and offering your time. Identify and list down those to whom you would like to contribute.

____

____

____

____

____

____

____

____

Contribute to society, a specific community, an NGO, or a specific family or person for the next 3 months, and take note of the impact it has on your life.

____

____

____

____

____

____

____

____

____

____

____

Encourage others to embrace the act of "sharing" and work towards fostering a strong and vibrant community around you.

____

____

____

____

____

____

____

____

____

____

____

Chapter 11, 9 Secrets don't work unless...

Congratulations! You did it! You have learned 9 powerful secrets that can help you achieve your desired goals in life. How do you feel now? Are you excited? Do you believe that these 9 secrets can truly aid you in reaching your goals? Countless participants in my webinars and seminars have expressed their confidence in these secrets and how they have helped them achieve their goals. They have described it as nothing short of amazing!

Most individuals typically engage in writing, affirming, and visualizing their goals. However, only a few express gratitude throughout the manifestation process when affirming their goals. Surprisingly, no one seems to utilize all nine secrets simultaneously. In general, people tend to overlook the importance of truly feeling their affirmations, and they fail to adopt an effective gesture that facilitates the easy manifestation of their goals. Furthermore, they are unaware of the power that rhymes and rhythms hold. Additionally, they lack knowledge about the individual power each secret possesses, as well as the combined power that emerges when all nine secrets are utilized together.

How I discovered 9 secrets?

During my learning journey, I wasn't taught these 9 secrets in any particular order. I read numerous books on personal development and attended various workshops, eventually uncovering these 9 secrets along the way. I meticulously recorded every piece of information and then pieced them all together, like solving a jigsaw puzzle.

One book and workshop taught me the power of meditation, while another emphasized the power of visualization. Some books and workshops discuss the magic of gratitude, while a few others emphasize the importance of writing goals. Have you had similar experiences? In the past, I would follow the instructions provided in each book or workshop. I used to feel confused and would select one approach from each source to pursue my goals, abandoning the previous one once I discovered another.

When I first started writing affirmations to manifest my desired results, I neglected my meditation practice. I was unsure how to incorporate affirmations into my meditation routine and didn't understand the connection between writing affirmations and feeling them simultaneously. Additionally, I didn't write affirmations at all when I began using physiology. I had all the necessary pieces to achieve my goals, but they were scattered and I didn't know how to bring them together. I struggled to find the specific modality that would help me achieve my goals. Did you feel the same way a few years ago? I eventually learned that all modalities have their merits. Each author describes their own modality based on their personal experiences, and none of them are incorrect. Many people have benefited from these tools and techniques. However, I didn't achieve the desired results even after learning and using various modalities separately. I diligently practiced meditation, which brought me peace of mind and clarity of thoughts. I was able to change my basic nature, but I couldn't figure out how to integrate meditation with affirmations and visualization. I also didn't know how to combine gratitude practice with visualization or how a simple gesture could alter neurological pathways.

I have been writing affirmations for many years, but I didn't know how to integrate them with the power of "Gratitude," add vibrational words to the affirmations, and truly "Feel" them. As a result, I was only doing a fraction of the entire process at a time, without even realizing it. Consequently, I didn't achieve the extraordinary results in my life that I desired. I lacked confidence in my ability to easily and quickly achieve everything I wanted through these modalities that I had learned. The more confused I became, the more modalities I learned out of curiosity. Have you faced a similar situation? Guess what happened to me! I stopped using all the modalities. I neither used affirmations nor meditated anymore, and unsurprisingly, I didn't achieve the desired results. I lost faith in these modalities and believed that they were only possible for certain people, not for me. I concluded that everything I had learned and understood was merely philosophy and not practically implementable in my life. If it did work, I considered the person lucky enough to have achieved their goals. I literally gave up on all of them. I was resigned.

And suddenly, one day, I had an idea. I decided to compile all the modalities I had learned and practiced separately onto one sheet of paper. To my amazement, I was able to identify the connections among these modalities and see the bigger picture. My mind created new neurological pathways for each modality, revealing the 9 secrets of success. With this newfound understanding of their relationship, I was excited to apply these 9 secrets to manifest my desired results in life. I started teaching these secrets to others, who found them valuable and logical. As I continued to teach and practice all 9 secrets, my participants and I experienced happiness.

The Science of "Being"

Although I teach, promote, and practice the 9 secrets, I have not experienced any extraordinary results. The science behind these secrets is sound and makes complete sense, but I have not seen results. To investigate further, I began to survey my participants across different areas of their lives, and I discovered similar outcomes. Some participants who practiced the 9 secrets achieved temporary results, but they were unable to attain the level of happiness and contentment they desired. They found that they could modify their actions and consequently alter their results, but there was no transformation in their core "Being". They realized that they could be a happy "Being" for one person and an unhappy one for another, or succeed in one aspect of life while failing in another, all at the same time. The challenge arose from the fact that their fundamental behaviors and mindsets remained unchanged..

I was amazed to discover that the same results I observed in my own life were also evident in many of my students who practiced the 9 secrets! Through this practice, I was able to temporarily create new neurological pathways. In the past, I would react negatively and perform poorly when faced with adversity or difficult individuals. My behavior would vary depending on the situation, whether it was favorable or unfavorable. I was not consistent in how I acted with different people - my "Being" would constantly change. For instance, I could achieve remarkable success and happiness in my business, while simultaneously experiencing unhappiness and failure in my relationships. I would be warm and loving with my family, yet frustrated and upset with my colleagues at work.

9 secrets helped me achieve a specific goal temporarily, but they didn't have a positive impact on other areas of my life where I wanted consistent results. Why is that? Why don't these 9 secrets

work all the time? So I delved deeper and discovered the "5-step formulas."

I was amazed when I discovered the 5-step formula. It helped me understand the reasons why I wasn't achieving the desired results in life, despite practicing the 9 secrets of the subconscious mind. I started working on the 5 steps individually and, surprisingly, began seeing better results in my life. What's more, I regained my peace of mind, which has allowed me to generate more creative ideas for achieving my goals. Now, I am able to take actions effectively.

In my next book, I will share with you a proven 5-step formula and the scientific reasoning behind it, so that you can achieve your goals. By using this formula, your mind has the ability to create new neurological pathways, allowing you to achieve the desired outcomes with confidence, ease, and effectiveness.

The 5-step formula will assist you in recognizing and transforming your limiting beliefs. By understanding and implementing these steps, you will be able to cultivate new and empowering beliefs.

Get ready to experience long-lasting happiness, good health, and success in your life..

Chapter 11, Assignment

Note: Please write your answers or actions in the space provided after each task and make full use of it.

Make a list of the areas in your life where you have used "Affirmations" or other methods but have not seen significant improvements yet.

What affirmations have you been practicing for a long time without any positive results?

What is your existence or role in those areas of life? Take note of all of them.

9 Secrets at a Glance

I am so happy offer you this book, which serves as a comprehensive toolbox. It presents a 21-day challenge that allows you to concentrate on a specific goal in any area of your life. To achieve this goal, employ the science of affirmations by deliberately selecting positive thoughts, infusing them with emotions, and truly feeling the statement. Enhance the vibrancy of your affirmations by incorporating gratitude. Additionally, establish a physical gesture to hasten the manifestation of your affirmations. By meditating and channeling your emotions, visualize the outcomes you desire. Finally, write, sing, dance, and celebrate your affirmations to manifest your dreams easily and rapidly.

Create your own reality by applying all nine secrets for happiness and success. Start by focusing on one area for the next 21 days and practicing the 9 secrets. Once you see positive results in that area, apply the same formula to all other areas.

Pay attention to your thoughts, the words you speak, and the emotions you feel during manifestation. Practice consistently aligning them. Make it a lifelong habit - it's not just a 21-day challenge but a fundamental aspect of living.

If you don't intentionally focus your mind, it will naturally generate outcomes without your control. Make a conscious effort to engage in goal-oriented meditation, regularly practice your gestures, and foster a positive state of mind.

Discover why the 9 secrets fail and learn how to harness their power for faster manifestation of desired outcomes in the upcoming book, "Subconscious Mind."

If you have any questions about the assignment, feel free to email me directly at dipaali.pm@gmail.com. Best Wishes for your new & wonderful life!

My Books

Scan here to read.

Rewire Your Beliefs: Eliminate Limiting Beliefs, Stop Negative Thinking, Use Empowering Affirmations, and Transform Your Mind.

Scan here to read

Secrets of Happy Life - Conquer Your Inner World with Positive Self-talk. Master the Art of Forgiveness and Experience Joy. Fill Your Heart with Love and compassion.

Scan here to read

Everyday Happiness: 21 Tiny Habits to Conquer Your Stress, Experience Joy and Have a Content Life.

Scan here to read

7 Timeless Principles to Cultivate Love, Deepen Understanding, and Perpetuate Mutual Respect Among Loved Ones.

Scan here to read

66 Quick Prompts to Transcend Sadness, Embrace Happiness, Unveiling the Secrets to Lasting Joy.

Scan here to read

100 Powerful Thoughts to Empower Self-Confidence, Cultivate Resilience, and Illuminate the Path to Joyful

ABOUT AUTHOR

- Dipaali Ghanshyam Patel is a dedicated life coach, inner wellness advocate, and author passionate about transforming lives through mental health and happiness. Having overcome her own struggles with low self-esteem, negative thinking, and limiting beliefs, Dipaali discovered the power of continuous learning, meditation, and affirmations in reshaping her subconscious mind.

- Her personal journey from feeling unloved and unsupported to achieving profound personal breakthroughs inspires her mission to help others unlock their potential. Through her books, workshops, and online courses, Dipaali offers practical tools and techniques to identify and

eliminate subconscious limiting beliefs, empowering readers to create positive, fulfilling lives.

- With a commitment to promoting mental well-being, Dipaali teaches the art of meditation and the science of affirmations, guiding individuals to train their subconscious minds for lasting success and happiness.

- Join Dipaali's daily news later toknow her transformative journey to harness the power of your mind, overcome challenges, and design a life filled with joy and prosperity. Let her experiences and insights be your roadmap to a brighter, more empowered future. www.dipaali.life

BIG ASK

Visit my website and join my community for a transformative workshop that is ongoing and upcoming, where we will together spread INNER Purity into the outer world.

I kindly ask you to rate and write a review as an act of kindness. Your review holds importance to me and will positively impact humanity.

Google/Dipaali-life

www.ingramcontent.com/pod-product-compliance
Ingram Content Group UK Ltd.
Pitfield, Milton Keynes, MK11 3LW, UK
UKHW021937190726
13853UKWH00004B/1492